A Cowboy Christmas

A COWBOY CHRISTMAS

Celebrating the Season
on Ranch and Range

Edited by
Anne Tempelman-Kluit

Whitecap Books
Vancouver / Toronto

The information contained in this book is true and complete to the best of our
knowledge. All recommendations are made without guarantee on the part of the
editor or Whitecap Books Ltd. The editor and publisher disclaim any liability in
connection with the use of this information. For additional information please
contact Whitecap Books Ltd., 351 Lynn Avenue, North Vancouver, BC, V7J 2C4.

Every effort has been taken to trace the ownership of copyright material used in the
text. The editor and publisher welcome any information enabling them to rectify
any reference or credit in subsequent editions.

Copy-edited by Elizabeth McLean
Cover design by Tanya Lloyd and Graham Sheard
Interior design by Warren Clark
Front cover illustration by Val Lawton
Back cover and interior illustrations by Andrew Costen

Printed in Canada

Canadian Cataloguing in Publication Data
A cowboy christmas

  ISBN 1-55285-071-4

    1. Christmas—Literary collections. 2. Ranch life—Literary collections.
3. Cowboys—Literary collections. 4. American literature—20th century.
5. Canadian literature (English)—20th century.★
I. Tempelman-Kluit, Anne, 1941–
PN6071.C6C68 2000   810.8'0334   C00-910931-5

 The publisher acknowledges the support of the Canada Council for the Arts for our
publishing program and the Cultural Services Branch of the Government of British
Columbia in making this publication possible. We acknowledge the financial support
of the Government of Canada through the Book Industry Development Program for
our publishing activities.

For more information on other titles from
Whitecap Books, visit our web site at www.whitecap.ca

For Annemarie and Nadaleen,

for this and so much more—

and for Jane

Contents

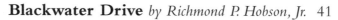
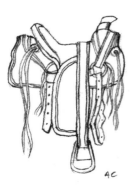

Introduction

Books have their beginnings in curious places. A snowy train trip through the Canadian Rockies sowed the seeds for this anthology. The early October snowstorm was unexpected and the foothills stretched smoothly white around us. From beside the tracks, elk watched the train pass and the man from New York was beside himself with excitement. Passengers took photographs, murmuring about Christmas cards. Out of the snow, two cowboys appeared, riding along the fold of a gentle hillside, their red bandannas bright on their otherwise monochromatic outfits. A black and white dog bounded along behind them, burying his nose in the snow and tossing the flakes into the air.

"Oh my," breathed the man from New York, "will you look at that."

Look we did, until they were out of sight. That image of the cowboys, their horses moving easily and leisurely through the snow, was in stark contrast to our mechanical transportation. My admiration for ranch hands, and indeed anyone who could ride a horse with confidence, grew. I recalled the first time I got on a horse, at a Cariboo dude ranch. I was appalled at how far it was to the ground. The horse seemed equally appalled at the graceless lump on his back and promptly headed back into the barn, despite my feeble efforts to convince him otherwise. We survived a two-hour trail ride and parted company with, I suspect, mutual relief.

At the end of my train trip, I visited a friend in Calgary. We ate ribs and chili in a cowboy restaurant, explored a cowboy heritage museum, bought a beetle-shaped boot scraper in a cowboy tack shop and looked at cowboy photographs at the Glenbow Museum. *A Cowboy Christmas* was born.

Researching cowboy stories was an entree into an enticing new world for me. From northern Alberta to New Mexico, cowboy poets gather together to tell poignant stories of loving and losing, but they also poke gentle fun at themselves. Cowhand humor is sometimes corny, sometimes black and almost always self-deprecating. Country and Western songs are unabashedly sentimental and the language of the cowboy is as unique as London Cockney slang. Chuckwagon cooking is, not surprisingly, simple and filling. Cowboy boots, saddles and hats have a mystique of their own. Time was when the cowboy paid more for his saddle than for his horse and craftsmen jealously guarded their intricate designs.

The spirit of the West for the urban cowboy may have almost nothing to do with real horses and cattle. The man in the ATM line-up may have never been near a barn, but the bounce in his step has nothing to do with his bank balance and everything to do with his red and black cowboy boots. You can dine off a dinner service with a Western theme or drive a car inset with rows of diamond-studded horseshoes. Clothing is brash and beautiful, from red satin and sequins to bold brass belt buckles and hand-tooled leather belts. Painted ties are avidly collected. Christmas tree ornaments include a tiny rhinestone cowboy complete with his own twinkling lights. Western sculpture and art has an enormous following, respect for the land and the animals evident in every piece.

But, cowboys are a tactiturn lot. Poems and songs were plentiful, stories were not. In my book *A Klondike Christmas*, most stampeders were spending their first Christmas away from home, and wrote about the contrast in their circumstances. In *A West Coast Christmas*, newcomers and travelers wrote home, or kept diaries, about their experiences in a new land. The old-time working cowboy, however, had spent many Christmases on the range, and saw no reason to chronicle the event. His was a life of loneliness and adversity, always on the move, always aware that his first concern must be for the cattle, whatever the weather and his own needs. His "home on the range" might be a desolate line-camp, far from even the meager comforts of the home ranch bunkhouse. He spent days herding the animals to richer feeding grounds, or weeks on the trail, driving them to market. Leisure time was rare. Small wonder that there are more fiction stories than diaries and reminiscences of life on the trail.

Still, despite the hardships of cowboyin', there were stories. In common with the lonely Gold Rush miner or West Coast logger, there was the urge to make some traditional celebration for Christmas, however bleak the circumstances, whether under a blazing Texas sun or in a British Columbia blizzard. In these stories outlaws risked capture, and each other, to spend a Christmas together. Men rode twenty miles on a frosty Christmas morning to check out the rumor of fresh doughnuts; women on remote ranches planned months ahead to make the day special for ranch hands and bachelor neighbors. Even the most cantankerous cowboy would contrive a toy from rope and wood for a lonely child and, sometimes, small miracles did happen.

Modern and early day cowboys are, at once and individually, swaggering, tough, generous, gentle, cynical, sentimental, loyal and hard-working. Today, the mystique and magic of life on the range survives as much in our imagination as in reality, but imagination is a powerful thing. It transforms what could be just another dreary December day into a festive celebration, with food and gifts fashioned by ingenuity and isolation—Christmas the cowboy way.

Shepherds of the Range

by S. Omar Barker

The lights shone gay that Christmas Eve. The dance had just begun,
With cowboys come from miles around, all fixed to have some fun.
The fiddler's foot was pattin' fast, the caller's voice sung out:
"Now swing your pardners, skin the coon and turn him wrong side out!"
'Twas music and 'twas laughter in the schoolhouse on the hill,
When from the bitter night outside a wailing shout rose shrill.
Quick stepped a cowboy to the door and swung it open wide.
In ragged clothing, white with snow, a chico stepped inside—
A Spanish kid with frightened face, his eyebrows rimmed with frost.
"May God have mercy, friends!" he cried. "My Tío Juan is lost
On Malpai Mesa with his sheep—the blizzard made them stray.
The cliffs along the rim are steep!" They let him have his say,
And though he spoke in Spanish, there were some that understood:
The kid had come to beg their help, yet feared 'twould do no good.

"Sheepherder lost?" One cowboy shrugged. "That don't spell me no woe!
On with the dance! It's Christmas Eve!" But another said: "Let's go!"
They rode aslant the driving storm with quip and joke and jest,
To where a craggy mesa loomed some five miles to the west.
Some damned the whole sheepherder tribe with many a hard-cussed name.
Some claimed 'twould be good riddance—but they rode on just the same.

They rode out in the bitter night, the warm lights left behind.
'Twas midnight when, with freezing feet, at last they made their find.
They found old Tío Juan alive and packed him in to thaw.
They rounded up what sheep they could to shelter in a draw.
"Well, damn sheepherders, anyhow! He spoilt our Christmas Eve!
We'll git back to the baile boys, just when it's time to leave!"
Thus grumbled one young cowhand, but the fiddler cut him short:
"I'll fiddle plumb to daylight if the women think I ort.
And as for cussin' shepherds, son, if I remember right,
Seems like it's in the Bible how they watched their flocks by night,
And when the Star of Bethlehem brung Christmas long ago,
The fellers first to see it—they was herdin' sheep, y'know!"

From *Rawhide Rhymes*

S. Omar Barker was just twenty when he began writing poetry in 1914. As well, his short stories have earned him a number of coveted awards, including the W.W.A. Spur Award for best Western short story in 1955. He is also the third person, and first living author, to be inducted into the newly established Hall of Fame of Great Western Writers in the National Cowboy Hall of Fame, Oklahoma City.

The Winter Camp:
Christmas is only another day at a cow camp

by Will James
Montana, about 1910

By the cottonwood-timbered creeks of the cow-country are scattered one- or two-roomed cabins which make up the cow-camps of every outfit.

The riders that stay with the outfit the year around are paired off to each camp where they're to ride through the winter and keep an eye on whatever stock which will need feeding; one or two "hay-shovelers" (ranch hands) are there to feed whatever stock the riders bring in. Sometimes there's a cook to help along in such camps, and as the winter sets in and the coulees fill up with drifts, the work accumulates till all hands are kept mighty busy. And the work goes on the same if the sun is shining or a blizzard is howling.

Christmas comes as just another day, and as the year dies out and the town folks are celebrating the coming of the new year, the rider is apt to be in some draw figgering ways to get around snowbanks with some little bunch of weak stock he's bringing in to camp.

From *All in the Day's Riding*

Born Joseph Ernest Nephtali Dufault in 1892, in Quebec, Canada, Will James traveled to the United States. He served in the army and also started to sell the sketches he had been drawing since he was four years old.

He later began writing; his most famous book, *Smoky*, was published in 1926. His last book, *The American Cowboy*, was published the year he died, in 1942. He divided his final years between his Montana ranch and a home in Billings, Montana.

Stubby Pringle's Christmas

by Jack Schaefer

High on the mountainside by the little line cabin in the crisp clean dusk of evening Stubby Pringle swings into saddle. He has shape of bear in the dimness, bundled thick against cold. Double socks crowd scarred boots. Leather chaps with hair out cover patched corduroy pants. Fleece-lined jacket with wear of winters on it bulges body and heavy gloves blunt fingers. Two gay red bandannas folded together fatten throat under chin. Battered hat is pulled down to sit on ears and in side pocket of jacket are rabbit-skin earmuffs he can put to use if he needs them.

Stubby Pringle swings up into saddle. He looks out and down over worlds of snow and ice and tree and rock. He spreads arms wide and they embrace whole ranges of hills. He stretches tall and hat brushes stars in sky. He is Stubby Pringle, cowhand of the Triple X, and this is his night to howl. He is Stubby Pringle, son of the wild jackass, and he is heading for the Christmas dance at the schoolhouse in the valley.

Stubby Pringle swings up and his horse stands like rock. This is the pride of his string, flop-eared ewe-necked cat-hipped strawberry roan that looks like it should have died weeks ago but has iron rods for bones and nitroglycerin for blood and can go from here to doomsday with nothing more than mouthfuls of snow for water and tufts of winter-cured bunchgrass snatched between drifts for food. It stands like rock. It knows the folly of trying to unseat Stubby. It wastes no energy in futile explosions. It knows that twenty-seven miles of hard winter going are foreordained for this evening and twenty-seven more of harder uphill return by morning. It has done this before. It is saving the dynamite under its hide for the destiny of a true cow pony which is to take its rider where he wants to go—and bring him back again.

Stubby Pringle sits his saddle and he grins into cold and distance and future full of festivity. Join me in a look at what can be seen of him despite the bundling and frosty breath vapor that soon will hang icicles on his nose. Those are careless haphazard scrambled features under the low hatbrim, about as handsome as a blue boar's snout. Not much fuzz yet on his chin. Why, shucks, is he just a boy? Don't make that mistake, though his twentieth birthday is still six weeks away. Don't make the mistake Hutch Handley made last summer when he thought this was young unseasoned stuff and took to ragging Stubby and wound up with ears pinned back and upper lip split and nose mashed flat and the whole of him dumped in a rain barrel. Stubby has been taking care of himself since he was orphaned at thirteen. Stubby has been doing man's work since he was fifteen. Do you think Hardrock Harper of the Triple X would have anything but an all-around hard-proved hand up here at his farthest winter-line camp siding Old Jake Hanlon, toughest hard-bitten old cowman ever to ride range?

Stubby Pringle slips gloved hand under rump to wipe frost off the saddle. No sense letting it melt into patches of corduroy pants. He slaps right-side saddle bag. It contains a burlap bag wrapped around a two-pound box of candy, of fancy chocolates with variegated interiors he acquired two months ago and has kept hidden from Old Jake. He slaps left-side saddlebag. It holds a burlap bag wrapped around a paper parcel that contains a close-folded piece of dress goods and a roll of pink ribbon. Interesting items, yes. They are

There's no place like home... (NA227-9)

ammunition for the campaign he has in mind to soften the affections of whichever female of the right vintage among those at the schoolhouse appeals to him most and seems most susceptible.

Stubby Pringle settles himself firmly into the saddle. He is just another of far-scattered poorly paid patched-clothes cowhands that inhabit these parts and likely marks and smells of his calling have not all been scrubbed away. He knows that. But this is his night to howl. He is Stubby Pringle, true begotten son of the wildest jackass, and he has been riding line through hell and high water and winter storms for two months without a break and he has done his share of the work and more than his share because Old Jake is getting along and slowing some and this is his night to stomp floorboards till schoolhouse shakes and kick heels up to lanterns above and whirl a willing female till she is dizzy enough to see past patched clothes to the man inside them. He wriggles toes deep into stirrups and settles himself firmly in the saddle.

"I could of et them choc'lates," says Old Jake from the cabin doorway. "They wasn't hid good," he says. "No good at all."

"An' be beat like a drum," says Stubby. "An' wrung out like a dirty dishrag."

"By who?" says Old Jake. "By a young un like you? Why, I'd of tied you in knots afore you knew what's what iffen you tried it. You're a dang-blatted young fool," he says. "A ding-busted dang-blatted fool. Riding out a night like this iffen it is Chris'mas Eve," he says. "But iffen I was your age agin, I reckon I'd be doing it too." He cackles like an old rooster. "Squeeze one of 'em for me," he says and he steps back inside and he closes the door.

Stubby Pringle is alone out there in the darkening dusk, alone with flop-eared ewe-necked cat-hipped roan that can go to the last trumpet call under him and with cold of wicked winter around him and with twenty-seven miles of snow-dumped distance ahead of him. "Wahoo!" he yells. "Skip to my Lou!" he shouts. "Do-si-do and round about!"

He lifts reins and the roan sighs and lifts feet. At easy warming-up amble they drop over the edge of benchland where the cabin snugs into tall pines and on down the great bleak expanse of mountainside.

Stubby Pringle, spurs ajingle, jogs upslope through crusted snow. The roan, warmed through, moves strong and steady under him. Line cabin and line work are far forgotten things back and back and up and up the mighty mass of mountain. He is Stubby Pringle, rooting tooting hard-working hard-playing cowhand of the Triple X, heading for the Christmas dance at the schoolhouse in the valley.

He tops out on one of the lower ridges. He pulls rein to give the roan a breather. He brushes an icicle off his nose. He leans forward and reaches to brush several more off sidebars of old bit in the bridle. He straightens tall. Far ahead, over top of last and lowest ridge, on into the valley, he can see tiny specks of glowing allure that are schoolhouse windows. Light and gaiety and good liquor and fluttering skirts are there. "Wahoo!" he yells. "Gals an' women an' grandmothers!" he shouts. "Raise your skirts and start askipping! I'm acoming!"

He slaps spurs to roan. It leaps like mountain lion, out and down, full into hard gallop downslope, rushing, reckless of crusted drifts and ice-coated bush branches slapping at them.

He is Stubby Pringle, born with spurs on, nursed on tarantula juice, weaned on rawhide, at home in the saddle of a hurricane in shape of horse that can race to outer edge of eternity and back, heading now for high jinks two months overdue. He is ten feet tall and the horse is gigantic, with wings, iron-boned and dynamite-fueled, soaring into forty-foot leaps down the flank of the whitened wonder of a winter world.

They slow at the bottom. They stop. They look up the rise of the last low ridge ahead. The roan paws frozen ground and snorts twin plumes of frosty vapor. Stubby reaches around to pull down fleece-lined jacket that has worked a bit up back. He pats right-side saddlebag. He pats left-side saddlebag. He lifts reins to soar up and over last low ridge.

Hold it, Stubby. What is that? Off to the right.

He listens. He has ears that can catch snitch of mouse chewing on chunk of bacon rind beyond the log wall by his bunk. He hears. Sound of axe striking wood.

AC.

What kind of dong-bonging ding-busted dang-blatted fool would be chopping wood on a night like this and on Christmas Eve and with a dance under way at the schoolhouse in the valley? What kind of chopping is this anyway? Uneven in rhythm, feeble in stroke. Trust Stubby Pringle, who has chopped wood enough for cookstove and fireplace to fill a long freight train, to know how an axe should be handled.

There. That does it. That whopping sound can only mean that the blade has hit at an angle and bounced away without biting. Some dong-bonged ding-busted dang-blatted fool is going to be cutting off some of his own toes.

He pulls the roan around to the right. He is Stubby Pringle, born to tune of bawling bulls and blatting calves, branded at birth, cowman raised and cowman to the marrow, and no true cowman rides on without stopping to check anything strange on range. Roan chomps on bit, annoyed at interruption. It remembers who is in saddle. It sighs and obeys. They move quietly in dark of night past boles of trees jet black against dim grayness of crusted snow on ground. Light shows faintly ahead. Lantern light through a small oiled-paper window.

Yes. Of course. Just where it has been for eight months now. The Henderson place. Man and woman and small girl and waist-high boy. Homesteaders. Not even fools, homesteaders. Worse than that. Out of their minds altogether. All of them. Out here anyway. Betting the government they can stave off starving for five years in exchange for one hundred sixty acres of land. Land that just might be able to support seven jackrabbits and two coyotes and nine rattlesnakes and maybe all of four thin steers to a whole section. In a good year. Homesteaders. Always out of almost everything, money and food and tools and smiles and joy of living. Everything. Except maybe hope and stubborn endurance.

Stubby Pringle nudges the reluctant roan along. In patch light from the window by a tangled pile of dead tree branches he sees a woman. Her face is gray and pinched and tired. An old stocking cap is pulled down on her head. Ragged man's jacket bumps over long woolsey dress and clogs arms as she tries to swing an axe into a good-sized branch on the ground.

Whopping sound and axe bounces and barely misses an ankle.

"Quit that!" says Stubby, sharp. He swings the roan in close. He looks down at her. She drops axe and backs away, frightened. She is ready to bolt into two-room bark-slab shack. She looks up. She sees that haphazard scrambled features under low hatbrim are crinkled in what could be a grin. She relaxes some, hand on door latch.

"Ma'am," says Stubby. "You trying to cripple yourself?" She just stares at him. "Man's work," he says. "Where's your man?"

"Inside," she says; then, quick, "He's sick."

"Bad?" says Stubby.

"Was," she says. "Doctor that was here this morning thinks he'll be all right now. Only he's almighty weak. All wobbly. Sleeps most of the time."

"Sleeps," says Stubby, indignant. "When there's wood to be chopped."

"He's been almighty tired," she says, quick, defensive. "Even afore he was took sick. Wore out." She is rubbing cold hands together, trying to warm them. "He tried," she says, proud. "Only a while ago. Couldn't even get his pants on. Just fell flat on the floor."

Stubby looks down at her. "An' you ain't tired?" he says.

"I ain't got time to be tired," she says. "Not with all I got to do."

Stubby Pringle looks off past dark boles of trees at last low ridgetop that hides valley and schoolhouse. "I reckon I could spare a bit of time," he says. "Likely they ain't much more'n started yet," he says. He looks again at the woman. He sees gray pinched face. He sees cold shivering under bumpy jacket. "Ma'am," he says. "Get on in there an' warm your gizzard some. I'll chop you a bit of wood."

Roan stands with dropping reins, ground-tied, disgusted. It shakes head to send icicles tinkling from bit and bridle. Stopped in midst of epic run, wind-eating, mile-gobbling, iron-boned and dynamite-fueled, and for what? For silly chore of chopping.

Fifteen feet away Stubby Pringle chops wood. Moon is rising over last low ridgetop and its light, filtered through trees, shines on leaping blade. He is Stubby Pringle, moonstruck maverick of the Triple X, born with axe in hands, with strength of stroke in muscles, weaned on whetstone, fed on cordwood, raised to fell whole forests. He is ten feet tall and axe is enormous in moonlight and chips fly like stormflakes of snow and blade slices through branches thick as his arm, through logs thick as his thigh.

He leans axe against a stump and he spreads arms wide and he scoops up whole cords at a time and strides to door and kicks it open...

Both corners of front room by fireplace are piled full now, floor to ceiling, good wood, stout wood, seasoned wood, wood enough for a whole wicked winter week. Chore done and done right, Stubby looks around him.

Fire is burning bright and well-fed, working on warmth. Man lies on big old bed along opposite wall, blanket over, eyes closed, face gray-pale, snoring long and slow. Woman fusses with something at old woodstove. Stubby steps to doorway to back room. He pulls aside hanging cloth. Faint in dimness inside he sees two low bunks and in one, under an old quilt, a curly-headed small girl and in the other, under another old quilt, a boy who would be waist-high awake and standing. He sees them still and quiet, sleeping sound. "Cute little devils," he says.

He turns back and the woman is coming toward him, cup of coffee in hand, strong and hot and steaming. Coffee the kind to warm the throat and gizzard of chore-doing hard-chopping cowhand on a cold cold night. He takes the cup and raises it to his lips. Drains it in two gulps. "Thank you, ma'am," he says. "That was right kindly of you." He sets cup on table. "I got to be getting along," he says. He starts toward outer door.

He stops, hand on door latch. Something is missing in two-room shack. Trust Stubby Pringle to know what. "Where's your tree?" he says. "Kids got to have a Christmas tree."

He sees the woman sink down on chair. He hears a sigh come from her. "I ain't had time to cut one," she says.

"I reckon not," says Stubby. "Man's job anyway," he says. "I'll get it for you. Won't take a minute. Then I got to be going."

He strides out. He scoops up axe and strides off, upslope some where small trees climb. He stretches tall and his legs lengthen and he towers huge among trees, swinging with ten-foot steps. He is Stubby Pringle, born an expert on Christmas trees, nursed on pine needles, weaned on pine cones, raised with an eye for size and shape and symmetry. There. A beauty. Perfect. Grown for this and for nothing else. Axe blade slices keen and swift. Tree topples. He strides back with tree on shoulder. He rips leather whangs from his saddle and lashes two pieces of wood to tree bottom, crosswise, so tree can stand upright again.

Stubby Pringle strides into shack, carrying tree. He sets it up, center of front-room floor, and it stands straight, trim and straight, perky and proud and pointed. "There you are, ma'am," he says. "Get your things out an' start decorating. I got to be going." He moves toward outer door.

He stops in outer doorway. He hears the sigh behind him. "We got no things," she says. "I was figuring to buy some but sickness took the money."

Stubby Pringle looks off at last low ridgetop hiding valley and school-house. "Reckon I still got a bit of time," he says. "They'll be whooping it mighty late." He turns back, closing door. He sheds hat and gloves and bandannas and jacket. He moves about checking everything in the sparse front room. He asks her for things and the woman jumps to get those few of them she has. He tells her what to do and she does. He does plenty himself. With this and with that magic wonders arrive. He is Stubby Pringle, born to poverty and hard work, weaned on nothing, fed on less, raised to make do with least possible and make the most of that. Pinto beans strung on thread brighten tree in firelight and lantern light like strings of store-bought beads. Strips of one bandanna, cut with shears from sewing box, bob in bows on branch ends like gay red flowers. Snippets of fleece from jacket lining sprinkled over tree glisten like fresh fall of snow. Miracles flow from strong blunt fingers through bits of old paper bags and dabs of flour paste into link chains and twisted small streamers and two jaunty little hats and two smart little boats with sails.

"Got to finish it right," says Stubby Pringle. From strong blunt fingers comes five-pointed star, triple thickness to make it stiff, twisted bit of old wire to hold it upright. He fastens this to topmost tip of topmost bough. He wraps lone bandanna left around throat and jams battered hat on head and shrugs into now skimpy-lined jacket. "A right nice little tree," he says. "All you got to do now is get out what you got for the kids and put it under. I really got to be going." He starts toward outer door.

He stops in open doorway. He hears the sigh behind him. He knows without looking around the woman has slumped into old rocking chair. "We ain't got anything for them," she says. "Only now this tree. Which I don't mean it isn't a fine grand tree. It's more'n we'd of had 'cept for you."

Stubby Pringle stands in open doorway looking out into cold clean moonlit night. Somehow he knows without turning head two tears are sliding down thin pinched cheeks. "You go on along," she says. "They're good young uns. They know how it is. They ain't expecting a thing."

Stubby Pringle stands in open doorway looking out at last ridgetop that hides valley and schoolhouse. "All the more reason," he says soft to himself.

"All the more reason something should be there when they wake." He sighs too. "I'm a dong-bonging ding-busted dang-blatted fool," he says. "But I reckon I still got a mite more time. Likely they'll be sashaying around till it's most morning."

Stubby Pringle strides on out, leaving door open. He strides back, closing door with heel behind him. In one hand he has burlap bag wrapped around paper parcel. In other hand he has squarish chunk of good pine wood. He tosses bag parcel into lap folds of woman's apron.

"Unwrap it," he says. "There's the makings for a right cute dress for the girl. Needle-and-threader like you can whip it up in no time. I'll just whittle me out a little something for the boy."

Moon is high in cold cold sky. Frosty clouds drift up there with it. Tiny flakes of snow float through upper air. Down below by a two-room shack droops a disgusted cow-pony roan, ground-tied, drooping like a statue snow-crusted. It is accepting the inescapable destiny of its kind which is to wait for its rider, to conserve deep-bottomed dynamite energy, to be ready to race to the last margin of motion when waiting is done.

Inside the shack fire in fireplace cheerily gobbles wood, good wood, stout wood, seasoned wood, warming two rooms well. Man lies on bed, turned on side, curled up some, snoring slow and steady. Woman sits in rocking chair, sewing. Her head nods slow and drowsy and her eyelids sag weary but her fingers fly, stitch-stitch-stitch. A dress has shaped under her hands, small and flounced and with little puff sleeves, fine dress, fancy dress, dress for smiles and joy of living. She is sewing pink ribbon around collar and down front and into fluffy bow on back.

On a stool nearby sits Stubby Pringle, piece of good pine wood in one hand, knife in other hand, fine knife, splendid knife, all-around-accomplished knife, knife he always has with him, seven-bladed knife with four for cutting from little to big and corkscrew and can opener and screwdriver. Big cutting

blade has done its work. Little cutting blade is in use now. He is Stubby Pringle, born with feel for knives in hand, weaned on emery wheel, fed on shavings, raised to whittle his way through the world. Tiny chips fly and shavings flutter. There in his hands, out of good pine wood, something is shaping. A horse. Yes. Flop-eared ewe-necked cat-hipped horse. Flop-eared head is high on ewe neck, stretched out, sniffing wind, snorting into distance. Cat hips are hunched forward, caught in crouch for forward leap. It is a horse fit to carry a waist-high boy to uttermost edge of eternity and back.

Stubby Pringle carves, swift and sure. Little cutting blade makes final little cutting snitches. Yes. Tiny mottlings and markings make no mistaking. It is a strawberry roan. He closes knife and puts it in pocket. He looks up. Dress is finished in woman's lap. But woman's head has dropped down in exhaustion. She sits slumped deep in rocking chair and she too snores slow and steady.

Stubby Pringle stands up. He takes dress and puts it under tree, fine dress, fancy dress, dress waiting now for small girl to wake and wear it with smiles and joy of living. He sets wooden horse beside it, fine horse, proud horse, snorting-into-distance horse, cat hips crouched, waiting now for waist-high boy to wake and ride it around the world.

Quietly he piles wood on fire and banks ashes around to hold it for morning. Quietly he pulls on hat and wraps bandanna around and shrugs into skimpy-lined jacket. He looks at old rocking chair and tired woman slumped in it. He strides to outer door and out, leaving door open. He strides back, closing door with heel behind. He carries other burlap bag wrapped around box of candy, of fine chocolates, fancy chocolates with variegated interiors. Gently he lays this in lap of woman. Gently he takes big old shawl from wall nail and lays this over her. He stands by big old bed and looks down at snoring man. "Poor devil," he says. "Ain't fair to forget him." He takes knife from pocket, fine knife, seven-bladed knife, and lays this on blanket on bed. He picks up gloves and blows out lantern and swift as sliding moon shadow he is gone.

High high up frosty clouds scuttle across face of moon. Wind whips through topmost tips of tall pines. What is it that hurtles like hurricane far down there on upslope of last low ridge, scattering drifts, smashing through brush, snorting defiance at distance? It is flop-eared ewe-necked cat-hipped roan, iron-boned and dynamite-fueled, ramming full gallop through the dark of night. Firm in saddle is Stubby Pringle, spurs ajingle, toes atingle, out on prowl, ready to howl, heading for the dance at the schoolhouse in the valley. He is ten feet tall, great as a grizzly, and the roan is gigantic, with wings, soaring upward in thirty-foot leaps. They top out and roan rears high, pawing stars out of sky, and drops down, cat hips hunched for fresh leap out and down.

Hold it, Stubby. Hold hard on reins. Do you see what is happening on out there in the valley?

Tiny lights that are schoolhouse windows are winking out. Tiny dark shapes moving about are horsemen riding off, are wagons pulling away.

Moon is dropping down the sky, haloed in frosty mist. Dark gray clouds dip and swoop around sweep of horizon. Cold winds weave rustling through ice-coated bushes and trees. What is that moving slow and lonesome up snow-covered mountainside? It is a flop-eared ewe-necked cat-hipped roan, just that, nothing more, small cow pony, worn and weary, taking its rider back to clammy bunk in cold line cabin. Slumped in saddle is Stubby Pringle, head down, shoulders sagged. He is just another of far-scattered poorly paid patched-clothes cowhands who inhabit these parts. Just that. And something more. He is the biggest thing there is in the whole wide roster of the human race. He is a man who has given of himself, of what little he has and is, to bring smiles and joy of living to others along his way.

He jogs alone, slump-sagged in saddle, thinking of none of this. He is thinking of dances undanced, of floorboards unstomped, of willing women left unwhirled.

He jogs along, half-asleep in saddle, and he is thinking now of bygone Christmas seasons and of a boy born to poverty and hard work and make-do poring in flicker of firelight over ragged old Christmas picture book. And suddenly he hears something. The tinkle of sleigh bells.

Sleigh bells?

Yes, I am telling this straight. He and roan are weaving through thick-clumped brush. Winds are sighing high overhead and on up the mountainside and lower down here they are whipping mists and snow flurries all around him. He can see nothing in mystic moving dimness. But he can hear. The tinkle of sleigh bells, faint but clear, ghostly but unmistakable. And suddenly he sees something. Movement off to the left. Swift as wind, glimmers only through brush and mist and whirling snow, but unmistakable again. Antlered heads high, frosty breath streaming, bodies rushing swift and silent, floating in flash of movement past, seeming to leap in air alone needing no touch of ground beneath. Reindeer? Yes. Reindeer strong and silent and fleet out of some far frozen northland marked on no map. Reindeer swooping down and leaping past and rising again and away, strong and effortless and fleeting. And with them, hard on their heels, almost lost in swirling snow mist of their passing, vague and formless but there, something big and bulky with runners like sleigh and flash of white beard whipping in wind and crack of long whip snapping.

Startled roan has seen something too. It stands rigid, head up, staring left and forward. Stubby Pringle, body atingle, stares too. Out of dark of night ahead, jingled with moan of wind, comes a long-drawn chuckle, deep deep chuckle, jolly and cheery and full of smiles and joy of living. And with it long-drawn words.

"We-e-e-l-l-l do-o-o-ne...pa-a-a-art-ner!"

Stubby Pringle shakes his head. He brushes an icicle from his nose. "An' I didn't have a single drink," he says. "Only coffee an' can't count that. Reckon I'm getting soft in the head." But he is cowman through and through, cow-man through to the marrow. He can't ride on without stopping to check anything strange on his range. He swings down and leads off to the left. He fumbles in jacket pocket and finds a match. Strikes it. Holds it cupped and bends down. There they are. Unmistakable. Reindeer tracks.

Stubby Pringle stretches up tall. Stubby Pringle swings into saddle. Roan needs no slap of spurs to unleash strength in upward surge, up up up steep mountainside. It knows. There in saddle once more is Stubby Pringle, moonstruck maverick of the Triple X, all-around hard-proved hard-honed cowhand, ten feet tall, needing horse gigantic, with wings, iron-boned and dynamite-fueled, to take him home to little line cabin and some few winks of sleep before another day's hard work....

Stubby Pringle slips into cold clammy bunk. He wriggles vigorous to warm blanket under and blanket over.

"Was it worth all that riding?" comes voice of Old Jake Hanlon from other bunk on other wall.

"Why, sure," says Stubby. "I had me a right good time."

All right, now. Say anything you want. I know, you know, any dong-bonged ding-busted dang-blatted fool ought to know, that icicles breaking off branches can sound to drowsy ears something like sleigh bells. That blurry eyes half asleep can see strange things. That deer and elk make tracks like those of reindeer. That wind sighing and soughing and moaning and maundering down mountains and through piney treetops can sound like someone shaping words. But we could talk and talk and it would mean nothing to Stubby Pringle.

Stubby is wiser than we are. He knows, he will always know, who it was, plump and jolly and belly-bouncing, that spoke to him that night out on wind-whipped winter-worn mountainside.

"We-e-e-l-l-l do-o-o-ne…pa-a-a-art-ner!"

From *Christmas Out West*
"Stubby Pringle's Christmas" was originally written as a children's story, but it has become a Western classic and is considered to be the best Western Christmas story ever by many. Jack Schaefer, who had a life-long interest in Western history, was a prolific writer of Western short stories and novels. His best-known book is probably *Shane*.

Campfire Coffee

Fill a coffee pot with fresh, cold water to just below the spout. Add one tablespoon of ground coffee for every cup of water and one more for the pot. Throw in a well-crushed eggshell and a pinch of salt (optional). Set over fire and bring to a boil. Remove from heat and allow grounds to settle before pouring.

Cowboys have a saying that if you throw a horseshoe into the pot and it doesn't float, the coffee isn't strong enough!

The Bull Named Jimmy Hoffa

by Paul St. Pierre
Merritt, B.C.

To get a muley Hereford bull named Jimmy Hoffa home for Christmas at the Guichon Ranch required five men, two horses, two snowmobiles, one truck, one airplane, and twelve days. You and I may be glad that we don't own that bull. If you're not, I am.

The Jimmy Hoffa affair began around Thanksgiving Day. By that time the winter snows were settling on the Guichon summer range and sixty-one of their sixty-two bulls had made their own way out of the high country and down to the home ranch at the upper end of Nicola Lake. There the cattle winter on bales of hay and their private thoughts.

By November 1 the bull Jimmy Hoffa was still absent. Gerard Guichon and his son Lawrie were mildly perturbed. Jimmy Hoffa was bought last year in Lethbridge, Alberta. He was one of the least intellectual sons of Lethbridge and knew nothing about mountains.

Two cowboys, Joe Pete and Jimmy Michael of Quilchena Reserve, spent the first week of November in the hills, tiring their saddle horses in the deepening snows. They didn't find him.

On November 11 Lawrie Guichon, who is also a commercial pilot, rented a Cessna 180 from Kamloops. He, his father, Joe Pete, and ranch mechanic Scott MacMillan flew the hills and valleys of the summer range.

Joe Pete spotted Jimmy Hoffa at the shore of Michel Lake, standing disconsolate in the snow. Michel Lake is about fifteen miles from the home ranch on the wrong side of a high ridge.

On November 12 Lawrie, Joe, and Scott left the ranch at 8:30 a.m. in a truck, packing two Skidoo Alpine Double Track snowmobiles. When the snow became too deep for the truck they unloaded the snowmobiles and set off for the ridge, carrying sandwiches for themselves and one bale of hay for Jimmy Hoffa.

They found him standing in three feet of snow at the lakeshore about 1:30 p.m.

He had eaten all the swamp grass left uncovered by snow and had turned to chewing willow twigs. He had slimmed down from his normal 2200 pounds to about 1900. He was sulky.

They fed him. Then, one snowmobile behind, one ahead with a man throwing handfuls of hay over his shoulder, they induced Jimmy Hoffa to start down the trail for home.

The bull traveled only about a mile. Shortly before dark the men left him with the rest of the hay and made their own way back to the ranch-house.

November 13 they went back at dawn in the snowmobiles, one of which broke and had to be repaired with haywire and prayer. The bull had returned to Michel Lake. That day they coaxed him as far as Frogmore Lake and again, dark approaching, left him.

November 14 they prodded Jimmy Hoffa 1000 feet up to the Frogmore Ridge, from which he might look down upon the warm valley of the Nicola where the winter feed was stacked waiting for him. A carburetor on one snowmobile had to be repaired that day.

The Quilchena Hotel was built in 1908, the adjoining General Store in 1913. Closed in 1917 because of prohibition, it was reopened in 1958 by Guy Rose, grandson of Joseph Guichon, Jr. Mr. Rose also owns part of the original Guichon ranch, which is still a working cattle ranch.

November 15 they returned at dawn to find that Jimmy Hoffa had come down from the ridge, but the wrong way. He had headed back for Frogmore Lake and starvation. They got him up and over the ridge again.

November 16 Pete, on saddle horse, brought him the rest of the way home where he now eats hay instead of snow and treats the other sixty-one bulls with ill-concealed hostility.

Jimmy Hoffa is not the bull's real name. He is a purebred with a long name registered in the Canadian livestock records. The Guichons call him Jimmy Hoffa because he doesn't do much work himself but he prevents others from getting their work done.

From *Chilcotin Holiday*
Most of the stories in this book first appeared as columns in the *Vancouver Sun*. St. Pierre traveled widely in British Columbia and wrote with humor and compassion about the people and places he visited. He was also the Chilcotin's Member of Parliament.

Standing Alone in the Darkness

by Arthur Winfield Knight

St. Joseph
Missouri
Christmas Day, 1881

Dear Susan,

Billy the Kid was killed five months ago.

Two months ago there was a gunfight in Tombstone, Arizona. It only lasted thirty seconds, but when it was over, three men were dead and another two were badly wounded.

Wyatt Earp and two of his brothers, along with a dentist named Holliday, shot it out with the Clanton-McLaury faction at the O.K. Corral. Some people claim the Earps opened fire without giving the others a chance, but you know what people say about me. It's hard to determine the truth, even about yourself.

Sometimes I think an era's coming to an end.

Sometimes I'll walk down the hill toward the site of the old Pony Express station. It's been gone more than twenty years. They claim they could have galloped around the world twenty-four times in the year and a half they existed. And now the stables are boarded up and weeds are growing through the cracks in the cobblestones out front. I stand there, trying to bring it all back: the smell of the horses and the hay, the men sweating, but it's all gone. Like the twins. Like Cole. Like so many things.

Gone.

The street down the road from our house is covered with snow. I look down the long hill from our house in the twilight; the sky looks like a bloody rose, getting redder and redder. I think it's going to burst into flame, the clouds shriveling up like burning petals, but the light just gradually fades, the way our lives do.

The snow looks like it's on fire. Outside, Jesse Jr. and Mary are making a snowman. He has eyes made out of lumps of coal and a carrot for a nose.

For a while, I helped with the snowman, but I'm more sensitive to cold than I used to be, and there's a pain behind my eyes that never goes away unless I take enough morphine.[...]

Last night, I dressed up in a Santa Claus suit. The kids and Zee had just finished decorating the tree when I came into the front room. "Ho, ho, ho, what have we here?" I asked.

"Daddy, Daddy, you look funny," little Jesse cried.

"I told you it was a dumb idea," Bob said.

I just ignored him, though.

We turned down the lanterns until the wicks were almost smoking, then we lit the candles on the tree and exchanged presents. Mary tried to eat the paper her jacks were wrapped in, but little Jesse took it away from her and said, "No, you don't eat that." I could tell it made him feel grown-up, counseling a two-year-old.

I've been trying to remember what it was like when we were kids. I know we weren't moving from place to place—there was a sense of stability in our lives—and we weren't friendless. Perhaps this life hasn't damaged Jesse or Mary yet, but we can't keep moving the way we have been.

There's a farm for sale near Lincoln, Nebraska. If I can raise the money, I'd like to buy it. ("Just one more job," I tell Zee. "That's why I need Bob.") Maybe we can finally stop running. You and Allen have done it. And it looks like Frank has. Why can't I?

Next year my son will be in first grade, and I want him to have a normal life. It's something I pray for.

After the presents were opened, we stood around the tree. Even Bob did, although I had to nudge him. If they ever make a play out of A Christmas Carol, *they can get Bob to play Scrooge.*

Zee and I held hands and we began singing. "It came upon a midnight clear, / That glorious song of old." Our voices rose and fell. Rose and fell. "From angels bending near the earth, / To touch their harps of gold."

Bob stood there, moving his lips a little, but I could tell he wasn't singing.

At the end of the song there was something about peace and good will, but no matter how hard I tried, I couldn't remember the words.

Maybe it was the morphine.

When Zee and the kids had gone to bed, Bob said, "I think I'll go out for a walk. Do you want to join me?"

"You go ahead, Bob."

I don't know why we've had him live with us. I guess it gives me someone to talk to now that I'm away from everyone I love—you, Frank, Ma—except Zee and the kids. Bob's like a dog. You could kick him and he'd wag his tail.

I get so lonely.... Sometimes I'll just sit, oiling my pistol and wiping it down. Counting the number of shells I have left. Sometimes I think that's about all I have left: bullets.

I sat next to the window, watching Bob disappear into the snow. It reminded me of the time I was visiting Belle in Texas. She and Cole and the rest of the folks had gone to bed and I was left to snuff out the candles on the Christmas tree. Seventeen years later, things end the same way.

I'm still standing alone in the darkness.

—Jesse

 From *Standing Alone in the Darkness*
The story of the outlaw Jesse James, as told in a series of fictional Christmas letters written between 1864 and 1881. Arthur Winfield Knight is well known for his books, plays and poems—many with an emphasis on famous, and infamous, Western historical people, including *Johnnie D.*, about the 1930s bank robber John Dillinger.

Wagon Boss Chili

2 pounds	lean round steak, cut into 1/2-inch cubes
2 tablespoons	canola oil
3	cloves garlic, minced
2 cups	chopped onions
1 cup	water
2 cups	beef broth
2 cups	canned tomatoes with juice, chopped
2 tablespoons	chili powder
1 teaspoon	dried oregano
1 teaspoon	ground cumin
1/2 teaspoon	cayenne pepper
1/2 teaspoon	salt
1/4 teaspoon	freshly ground black pepper
1 19-ounce can	pinto beans, rinsed and drained
3 tablespoons	cornmeal

In a Dutch oven, heat oil over medium-high heat. In several batches, cook beef, turning occasionally, for 5 minutes or until well-browned. Return all beef to saucepan, along with garlic and onions; cook for 5 minutes or until onions are tender.

Stir in the water, beef broth, tomatoes, chili powder, oregano, cumin, cayenne, salt and pepper. Bring to a boil, reduce heat to low and simmer, covered, for 2 hours or until meat is very tender.

Stir in beans and cornmeal; simmer for another 20 minutes or until mixture is heated through and thickened.

From *The Wild West Cookbook*
When cowboy cooks first put meat and peppers together, the seeds of modern-day chilis were sown and the West became the official domain of chili, hot sauces, searing salsas and "chiliheads."

The Matador Dance

by Lewis Atherton
Texas, 1882

Since the labor force on most ranches consisted almost wholly of unmarried men, the wives of resident owners or of resident managers largely determined the extent of organized social activities. As a consequence, this varied according to the personalities and interests of the women concerned. Spottswood Lomax, the first resident manager of the Spur Ranch, was born in Virginia, spent two years in Spain as a young man, and lived in St. Louis before migrating to Texas. His men respected him greatly throughout his tenure as manager from 1884 to 1889 because of his many fine qualities. Nevertheless, this tall, slender, sociable, soft-spoken, polished, educated and widely traveled manager made people around him feel somewhat inferior. Moreover, his wife disliked the isolation and privations of ranch life, and spent very little time at the Spur, preferring to move in Fort Worth society, where Lomax maintained a home for his family. Quite obviously, hands on the Spur Ranch could expect little formal social attention from the Lomaxes, and such was the case.

On the other hand, Mrs. H.H. Campbell, wife of the resident manager of the neighboring Matador, took an active interest in the social life of its cowboys, an interest which extended to hands from nearby ranches as well. From actual experience she and her husband knew how lonely ranch life could be. Starting out with virtually nothing and with little formal education, Campbell advanced rapidly in the cattle business. His wife, the former Lizzie Bundy, married him in 1871 and was a "neighbor" of Mrs. Goodnight when their husbands pioneered in the Texas Panhandle. Mrs. Campbell opened the Panhandle social whirl by giving a Christmas dance in 1882, and continued it

as an annual event until her husband severed connections with the owners of the Matador in 1890. In addition, she sponsored religious services for those who cared to attend.

Owen Wister's description of the pleasures derived from community dances in the cattle kingdom is substantiated in surviving accounts of Christmas dances on the Matador. Mrs. Campbell has been remembered as beautiful, capable, and dignified, with the accent of an aristocrat and a real fondness for the ranch hands. Whether she literally possessed all of those admirable traits or not, ranch hands obviously thought she did because of their appreciation for her kindnesses. At the first Matador Christmas dance in 1882, the six women present gathered from a distance of fifty miles in all directions. Over fifty men attended from the same region. Ben Brock, headquarters cook, and Bud Browning furnished the music, the latter being too religious to dance but not to fiddle for the better part of the two nights and a day that the gathering lasted. Annually, Mrs. Campbell prepared food to serve from fifty to one hundred people for a three-day period. After the first meal on the first night of the dance, people ate buffet style when they pleased

Two-horse open sleigh (NA2520-19)

for the remainder of their stay. Dancing went on almost constantly. When exhaustion compelled celebrants to drop out for an hour or two of sleep, women bedded down on the floor of the ranch house and men looked out for themselves. Quadrilles, waltzes, and schottisches were all popular. Mrs. Campbell forbade drinking and quarreling on such occasions and her wishes were generally respected. Everyone was welcome to come and many looked forward to the dance from one year to another.

From *The Cattle Kings*

Although much has been written about the romance of cowboying, little has been said about the role of the early cattlemen. These mostly young adventurers opened the plains, bringing prosperity, law and order to the Old West. Some were gentlemen farmers, while others were attracted by the challenge and rewards of cattle ranching.

Lewis Atherton, a history professor at the University of Missouri, and director of their Western History Manuscript Collection, has written several books and historical reviews about the Old West.

Drylander's Christmas

by S. Omar Barker

Four days before Christmas out on the Bar U
A case of the lonesomes had hit the whole crew.
Though mostly young fellers who'd drifted out West
Plumb off from their homefolks, it must be confessed
That comin' on Christmas, them lonesomes took hold.
As the dadblasted weather turned stormy and cold.
With the trail snowed too deep for a town gallyhoot.
Their chances for Christmas cheer weren't worth a hoot.
There'd be stock to tend to—some strays like as not —
And not much for Christmas but beans in a pot.

Now family homes in them days long ago
Was scattered plumb thin and as old-timers know
The feelin's 'twixt nesters and range-ridin' men
Was often plumb hostile. So here it had been
Till just before Christmas homesteader O'Toole
Took a notion that he'd put a boy on a mule
To spread the good word that on Christmas Eve night
His house would be warm, and with candles alight,
His missus and him would both welcome that crew
Of snowbounded cowhands out on the Bar U.
They said there'd be fixin's and maybe a chance
There might be some music and maybe some dance.

So the cowboys rode over in spite of the snow,
With the mercury hangin' about ten below.
Another farm family from off up the draw
Showed up in a wagon, not just pa and ma
But also three daughters. Believe it or not,
On that Christmas Eve all feuds was forgot!
And in that snug house on the drylander's claim
Five frostbitten cowhands were sure glad they came.
For the best Merry Christmas, them buckaroos found,
Is always the one where there's women around;
And if you ain't guessed it, 'twas Missus O'Toole
Who'd made the old man put that boy on a mule!

 S. Omar Barker had a checkered career
as an English professor, publicist for the
Las Vegas Cowboys Reunion, and as a
correspondent for the *Albuquerque
Journal* and the *Santa Fe New Mexican*.

He became a full-time writer in 1925,
when he was thirty-one, and his work
has appeared in more than one hundred
publications in the U.S., Canada and
Britain. As well, he wrote nine books
under the pseudonym Dan Scott.

Snowberries

by Susan Allison
Similkameen Valley, B.C., about 1870

Then began a busy time. It was now the first of November and the cattle and horses had to be driven to their winter quarters. My husband and his partner had about five hundred head of cattle to move that winter and a big bunch of horses, I don't know how many, I had not yet been introduced to them all. It took three or four busy days to gather them all and start them down the Canyon. Some of them would come back but the older ones just hit the trail and quietly grazed down the river and on to Okanagan, where their winter range was. It was a long journey in those days—but later, instead of going by Penticton and the lake, my husband cut a much shorter trail for his own use by Trout Creek. Of course, it was rough but answered his purpose.

When the bustle had subsided my husband set to work to make us comfortable for the winter, sawing logs that lay on the flat near the house for winter firewood. Then he hunted up what planks were left from house building and old tea boxes from which to make a desk, bureau, rocking chair and other articles of furniture we couldn't bring out. My sister had given me her old piano (the first one to enter B.C.) but as it could not then be packed over the Hope trail I left it with my mother. So we made the most of the few things we could get.

We were soon shut in by snow, our nearest neighbours at the Hudson's Bay Company post at Keremeos, forty miles down the valley. There were no

white settlers at Nicola, which place was named for the Great Head Chief, Incola, who claimed jurisdiction over the tribes of the Similkameen, Thompson, Shuswap, Okanagan, and even Kamloops. He died before I came into the country—but his memory was warm in the hearts of all the tribes he governed.

The Indians had gone to their winter quarters, either Nicola or Chu-chu-ewa. I found lots of amusement in making little things to make the house look pretty, and watching my husband carpentering. If he made a chair or couch I would make a covering for it. Then when Christmas came we gathered oregon-grape leaves for holly, and roseberries judiciously sewed in through the leaves looked like the berries. Snowberries took the place of mistletoe, and [we] had a jolly little Christmas dinner all to ourselves.

From *Pioneer of the Sixties*
Susan Moir was just fourteen in 1860 when she arrived in British Columbia from her native England. She and her family lived in Hope, Victoria and New Westminster before returning to Hope, where she helped her mother set up and run a small school.

In 1868 she married John Allison, for whom British Columbia's Allison Pass is named, and the newlyweds lived in the Similkameen Valley. The couple had fourteen children, but Susan Allison still found time to befriend her Indian neighbors and write down their legends. As well, she kept a journal of her day-to-day life, an invaluable record of the times.

Letter Home

by Herbert R. Hislop

Empire Ranch
Tucson
December 27, 1876

My dear Amy,

Many thanks for your letter which I received and read at 2 a.m. in the morning three days before Christmas and at the same time one from Marie and another from Mrs. Sweetland that were both very nice jolly letters. I have answered Marie's and I wrote to her at the same time as I wrote to you last and she has not yet received it. It is too bad if my letters get lost as most of them are long ones and take considerable time to write and I think most people know how I detest writing letters, but don't I like receiving them out here! Rather.

Well, "Christmas Day" has gone for another year and little did I think last Christmas that I should be out here this Christmas, and I am sure I do not know where I shall be next, but I should like to spend it in England. We spent our Christmas as merry as we could, we dined late that day and when all work was over, our sheep and horses corraled, we sat down to the festive meal, which I had taken great trouble to cook and serve as nicely and prettily as possible, not forgetting the familiar "Wishing you all a Merry Christmas" stuck in a stick at the top of the first successful plum-pudding at Empire Ranch, the inscription being in Spanish as well, so as our sheep herder could see it, but before he had finished he had to unbutton his waistcoat and the top button of another article of dress, finding that his eye was larger than his stomach. I surrounded the pudding with brandy and set light to it in the regular old style. Though we are in a rough country we try to enjoy ourselves sometimes, not being able to get a wild turkey we got 4 wild ducks, letting them hang for more than a week to give them a flavour and I stuffed and trussed these as best I could and I thought equal to a poulterer, only I had no sage and onions but plenty of breadcrumbs, salt, pepper and butter, a beautiful dish of nice brown mashed potatoes which I ornamented to the best of my ability, along with plum-pudding and brandy-sauce, good coffee and two bottles of whiskey the best we could get in the country. Of this our Christmas dinner consisted and no bad dinner either. I confess, though I cooked it all myself, that I have sat down to many a worse one, and that even out here, because I have sometimes never had the chance to sit down at all when I felt hungry and had lost my way. I could not procure all the articles necessary for the pudding but substituted them as best I could. In the place of beef suet I had to use mutton fat and could not procure either citron or lemons but in the place of lemons I put an orange and chopped up the peel. It was generally remarked that it was an excellent pudding and it was finished up the day after when cold, with the only regret that there was not any more. After dinner was over toasts were given, among which were "To Absent Friends," "To all our families," "To those we love." I suggested this one, as one of them forgot the name of his fiancée and so I put him out of his difficulty by suggesting the above, and last but not least I think, the "cook" as I certainly had taken a great deal of time and trouble, don't mention stoning the raisins. In honour of the day we altered our dress a little, all appearing at dinner with our coats on and hair brushed. I even put on a paper-collar and necktie and in fact almost considered myself full-dress, bar the knee-breeches and gaiters of course.

You seem to have been enjoying yourself very much at Windsor and to have been having a good time. I am glad that you have got your nerve back again to be able to ride in dog-carts and more especially behind fast horses. I used to think once that you never would drive with anyone again, but I am glad it is to the contrary. I have just been breaking a little mare for the saddle. She is very small only standing about 14 hands but as perfect and as pretty as any pony you could wish to see. She cost 5 pounds and can run pretty well and when broken thoroughly I am going to run her in a race, she is as quick as lightning. In this country they break horses with what they call a hackamoor, never using a bit at all. The hackamoor consists of a regular bridle and reins without a bit. It is not a pleasant sensation to feel yourself perched on a horse's back without any bit in its mouth, but it seems to break them very well as you only have to press the reins on the side of their neck and they will go which ever way you press so that you never use the bit like in England. I rather like it better as they are so easy to turn.

AC

Not far from our ranch a man killed a panther measuring 11 ft. from nose to tail. He shot it twice and thought he had killed it, but on going up discovered it was only wounded, and it sprang at him. He had a fight with it and eventually killed it but broke his rifle all to pieces. It is a good thing it is killed as it has been taking a good many sheep round here.

I wrote my last letter to you at the beginning of December hoping you would get it by Christmas Day but afterwards I feared whether it would be in time. In case the letter has miscarried I again wish you all the compliments of the season and a very Happy New Year to you all. Please to convey these sentiments also to the Fairbanks. I have sent my wishes in Marie's letter to the Romers, and so with best love to you all, hoping you are all well,

Believe me,
Your affec^{te} brother,
Herbert

From *An Englishman's Arizona: The Ranching Letters of Herbert R. Hislop 1876–1878*
The Empire Ranch, about 45 miles from Tucson, started small, but grew to become one of the largest in Arizona. Hislop, a wealthy young Englishman, first saw the ranch in 1876, in company with Walter Vail, who had also recently arrived in Tucson from Nevada. The two men went into partnership and bought the land.

Cowboy's Christmas

High River, Alberta
Christmas Day, 1893

Here in this land of the Wild West
Away from sweethearts and lovers,
Distant from the scenes of our childhood,
Away from our old-fashioned mothers,
Removed from the storm beaten cottage
Where the ivy still tenderly clings;
Our absence makes a broken circle,
Whilst we are like birds, on the wing.

Here in this land of the sunset,
Years have gone since we said adieu;
Yet Christmas recalls to our memories
The old faces and friends still true.
And tonight there's a depth of feeling,
Which unbidden thrills each breast,
Whilst we sing of the now broken circle,
Gathered in the old home nest.

They speak of our wild life on the plains;
How we laugh while storms are high,
While sharing our lot with the kine,
With our watchword to do or die,
They call us the wild daring cowboys,
Forgetting that 'neath the rough vest
The heart may beat tender as woman's,
Although with her charms unblessed.

Away then with dull care and sorrow;
The years are hastening away,
Why should we think of the morrow,
Why not drink and be merry today.
Then here's health to our dear old folks,
To the friends still loving and true;
Here's health to the land of our fathers,
And, Wild West, here's health to you.

From *Christmas in the West*
Nothing is known of the cowboy who
wrote this poem, which was written in
1893 and later appeared in the *Calgary
Tribune.*

Blackwater Drive

by Richmond P. Hobson, Jr.
West Central British Columbia, December 1939

The mercury was still creeping downwards. I knew that as night fell it was approaching sixty below zero. Our own chances, as well as those of the cattle, of surviving this night were running out on us. I thought: We could drop the cattle now and, as long as we were able to cross the Blackwater safely, we could make it to Pan Meadow and save our own hides.

But I shoved the thought out of my mind. We would stay with the cattle. We would never quit them.

As dark began to settle down around us I felt the fear of death gripping me. It was a strange sort of feeling. Then I worried about going suddenly crazy in the saddle—riding wildly in among the cattle, screaming and bellowing and waving my arms. The urge began to take hold of me—I tried to think clearly.

My brain must be getting frosted, I reasoned.

I pounded my beagle cap with my mittens. I kept punching and slapping the back of my head, my neck and my forehead. Gradually that strange feeling left me, and I was able to concentrate on what might lie ahead of us this frozen night—and on our chances of getting the cattle across the roaring Blackwater River.

As that cruel Christmas night deepened, I thought of other Christmas nights: of bright lights and warmth and laughter. Of cheerful greetings. Of music and sparkling jewelry and crystal chandeliers. Of women's soft voices. My mind drifted across the frozen snow-bound ranges towards my mysterious, blond girl—and I thought how I might never see her again.

I thought of homey places, crackling Christmas fires and gay people. Of children calling happily. I thought of another world, far away, of songs and

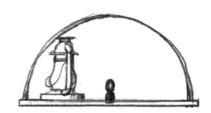

light and warmth and life. And then slowly—like the curtain on a stage—the black, silent night dropped around me.

A cow bawled somewhere in the snow behind, and far in the timbered distance the strange sad song of the wolf pack hovered for a moment, then sank into the silence of frozen forests.

Now a heavy, spruce-and-pine jungle stretched some four miles to the Blackwater crossing, where the trail crossed the river, zigzagged upwards for another four miles, climbing nearly a thousand feet in elevation above the Blackwater River to reach the Pan Meadow haystacks and cabin.

The fourteen-mile drive from the Chinee Lake pothole to the Pan Meadow was a long one under the best of circumstances, but with short days, and tired cattle fighting terrific cold and deep snow, it seemed almost impossible of accomplishment. But this was the only hope we had to save our cattle. There were no meadows here on the north side of the Blackwater between Chinee Lake and the crossing. There was no place for the cattle to pick for grass, or any openings large enough to hold them together and out of the timber.

If the cattle sneaked away from us before we crossed the river they would fan out north through the jungle and along the back trail for Batnuni. It would be an almost hopeless job to round them all up in the timber and herd them back to the crossing again—and I knew that few of them would ever make Batnuni.

On the start of the trip I had planned to push the cattle across the river, today, to a small opening below the Pan Meadow. I had figured that, with an early start and lots of good luck, we would have a fighting chance of crossing by dark. But I had not planned on the terrific cold, this deep snow, and played-out horses, men and cattle.

It seemed to me that the drive had plugged along in the dark for hours when I first heard the roar of the Blackwater rapids. It was a spine-tingling sound that carried with it the threat of disaster. I could feel my pulse quicken. The noise of the river deepened as we approached.

The tired lead cows suddenly stiffened and threw up their heads. This was a bad sign. I could vaguely make out the old, long-horned, brindle milk cow in the darkened trail ahead of me. She had stopped abruptly in her tracks, listening intently. Then she swung about and savagely flung her head and horns into a yearling immediately behind her. He plunged awkwardly to the side to avoid her attack. The frightened cow rushed into the bunched-up leaders.

This was dynamite. Cattle bawled along the back trail. I quirted Montana in at the horn-slashing cow. He crashed against the point of her shoulder. She almost went down—then skirted around me into the cows behind. I swung Montana about and beat the cow out as she plowed down the back trail scattering the cattle into the bush.

A sharp jackpine-stick missed my eye, took part of my eyebrow with it, and glanced off into space.

We got the crazy milk cow turned about in the trail. I figured Jimmy John was a half-mile behind me. Other cows and steers had turned about and were bawling contemplating a break down the back trail.

I was able to hold the line for a long minute. Then, using the same unexcited tone that my leaders were used to, I talked them into turning around and heading for the crossing. It was a close shave. If the front bunch

Winter crossing of the Bow River, Alberta (NA1047-1)

had made a real break for it and beat me out I don't want to think of what would have happened to the rest.

The Blackwater River was about three hundred feet wide at winter water levels, at the crossing. It plummeted at a dangerous speed over boulders and rocks, then plunged into a narrow, slow-moving, undertow lake. The crossing seldom freezes over until late in February.

Paul Krestenuk, a powerful, Russian-born, Indian trader, had, with the help of the Kluskus Indians, blazed and sunk sharp poles at intervals in the rushing water to serve as markers. If the water reached certain levels on those poles you knew whether the river could be crossed by teams and wagons, or only with saddle horses, or not at all. It was almost certain suicide to attempt the river if Paul's markers showed it to be too deep for saddle horses, for if a horse once lost its footing on the slippery rock bottom, and fell in the rapids, the current was so swift that the unfortunate animal seldom could struggle to his feet again. A number of Indians and white men have been drowned in the undertow of these still pools and roaring rapids. One of the victims was young Lashaway, a cousin of Jimmy John's, who had drowned three years before when his horse lost its footing and went down.[…]

The lead cattle broke from the timber out onto a wide chunk of snow-covered ice, and then stood solidly in their tracks, staring in wild-eyed panic at the black water that churned and frothed almost at their feet.

I rode hurriedly out to Krestenuk's markers. Montana cautiously approached the open river. The saddle-horse marker read passable. I looked off into the rushing channel. Spray was freezing in the air. Protruding boulders had turned to grotesque ice-topped figures.

The ice flats came to an abrupt end in nearly three feet of water. A big chunk of rotten ice had broken away from the bank and I could see signs of scraping hoofs and sleigh runners. The cavvy[1] and sleighs had obviously navigated the crossing.

But I realized that our chances of pounding cattle into the channel were very slim.

Cows were coming out on the sheet ice—bunching up—shoving and horning each other. I heard Jimmy John yell. I rode Montana through the back edge of the cattle and up alongside his dark form.

"Get these leaders into the water quick," snapped Jimmy, "before they've made up their minds!"

---

[1]Cavvy is a northwest cowboy term for a string of spare saddle horses or young horses in training that were taken along on the trail.

We rode in—a man and horse on each side of the stalled cows, our mounts pushing against the frightened animals.

For perhaps five minutes we talked trail talk, trying to persuade the cattle to make the cold plunge into the open water. But these tactics were a hopeless failure. Now there was only one thing to do—hit them hard—suddenly surprise them—get the first bunch stampeded into the river before they realized what had happened.

Aitkens rode up.

I had my long-barreled, 38.40 six-shooter strapped tight on the swell of my saddle. A couple of shots in the air above their heads would get a fast forward move out of the herd, but I knew the shots would spook the cattle behind us who were gradually drifting down the trail. That idea was out.

There was no use waiting for Simrose. He was perhaps a half-mile down the back trail moving the weaker animals in the drag. I called to Aitkens and Jimmy John:

"We're gonna hit them hard, boys. All the noise we can make—the wolf howls all together."

Slowly we drifted our horses back some twenty-five paces from the cattle which stood as if hypnotized.

"Give 'em hell!" I yelled.

We charged at full run into the hesitating herd with wild yells.

The river was perhaps thirty feet beyond the front line of critters. Some of them moved forward a few startled steps, then turned abruptly and started to mill.

This effort had failed. Now the bunch had swung about and were trying to get back off the ice into the timber.

"Hold them!" Jimmy yelled. "For God's sake, hold 'em out of the timber!"

We had to ride hard on the flanks of the cows to get them back onto the ice flats. Back and forth—in and out—forward—turn about—pivot here—plunge there. Gradually we worked the bunch into a great square body a few yards out from the timber.

Now I had to think fast. The sudden fight with the cows had warmed us vaguely, but the horses were weaker, and I knew the cattle had balked for keeps. We couldn't hold the herd on the icecap for long.

Simrose rode up out of the dark. He was mounted on Big Enough. The little, chunky bay was just what his name implied. He was as quick as a flash and plenty big enough. He shoved the last of the drag into the herd. Simrose knew at once what had happened. There was no time to waste.

"Rich," he called, "splash on to Pan Meadow. Get the other boys on fresh horses and bring us back a change ourselves. These cayuses can't take much more hard riding. We'll try and hold 'em here till you-all get back."

"O.K.," I yelled.

I swung the leg-weary Montana around the cattle and after some smooth talking and some gentle quirting he slid into the ice water. Spray hit my face. It felt warm. Montana didn't make that deep, hollow gasp that horses make when they drop suddenly into cold water. The icy river was warmer than the air.

The big gray felt his way cautiously out into the channel. I heard the Bear whimper and then saw him trotting along the ice upstream.

The water deepened to the saddle skirts. I quickly swung my feet forward onto Montana's neck. I held my breath. I knew that if my legs got dunked in the swim in this temperature, it would be all over but the shouting.

We were in the middle of the rapids now. Montana stumbled on a rock, started down to his knees. I saw the fast water coming up at me. But the cagey horse plunged forward again, almost went down, and then got his feet under him. We had been carried some distance below the crossing—a bit too far. The thin ice of the lake below the rapids with the river hurtling under it looked close enough to touch.

The timbered shore was coming closer. Montana broke through the ice on the bank. I took a deep frost-biting breath and dragged Montana around to look for the Bear. We didn't have to wait long. The loud-breathing cow-dog swept downstream to land at almost the exact spot we had. The smart old boy had made it across that river before and had learned from past experiences to enter the water far upstream in order to come out at the landing.

It was a long, uphill pull now. I trotted, then walked Montana. The black jackpines engulfed us, towered high into the glittering sky.

The dense forest was silent, forbidding. Occasionally a tree cracked in the distance. Far off and distinct now from the roar of the river, I could hear the pitiful bawls of the cattle.

Less than half an hour later Montana floundered out onto the great opening of the Pan Meadow. I caught a faint glimmer of light on the night horizon. In the distance a horse whinnied. Montana and I and the Bear had made the Pan Meadow, but three sick, half-frozen men, their horses, and three hundred cattle staggered dejectedly on the ice on the wrong side of the Blackwater River.

The dark bodies of horses churned and stomped about in piles of hay in the corral. Montana struggled up the slight incline towards the cabin light. I looked down at him. He was a frost-covered, ice-caked figure of a horse. I slipped off his back, staggered when I hit the snow, fell, then got to my feet and shoved through the door. A blast of heat struck me in the face. I almost fell again.

A single coal-oil lamp burned on a log table at the far corner of the room. A cast-iron heater roared out warmth. Buckets full of snow were thawing out on its surface.

Rob dragged about the cabin. Ed and Baxter lay half asleep on the floor. Stobie had a wet handkerchief over his eyes. He was propped against a bedroll in the corner.

Everyone looked up surprised.

"Cattle across O.K.?" asked Rob happily.

"No," I barked. "Cattle stalled on ice on far side. Can't move them. Get fresh horses for yourselves and changes for us. We've got to move fast."

[…]Now the boys were throwing on their sweaters and coats. They shoved out into the dark. Rob carried a lantern. I yelled after them:

"What the hell's the matter with you guys, sitting here in a warm cabin doing nothing!"

The door closed. I dipped a cup into the half-melted snow and took a long gulp. I had trouble rolling a smoke. I inhaled a few times—rubbed my hands together over the heater.

I felt lightheaded. Things were far away. The light was dim. I lay down on Baxter's bedroll on the floor. It seemed only a moment. Then someone had me by the shoulder and was shaking me. I opened my eyes. It was Rob.

"Get up and out, boy. Changed your riggin' to Stuyve. What the hell's the matter with you, laying here in a warm cabin doin' nothing?"

The Bear tried to follow me out the door. I knew he shouldn't swim the crossing again. He stood at the door—his head down. He didn't wag his tail. I told him we'd be back—then closed the door on him.

Again we rode into the frozen world—the silent darkness, the never-ending pain of the raw cold. Aching bodies—strange, ringing sounds in the ears. God, how sleepy we were!

[…]The roar of the river grew louder, drowning out the faraway bawls of the cattle. Now we dipped down the last of the inclines onto the flats and moved cautiously out on the icecap. Baxter rode ahead letting his horse pick its way. Rob and Ed and Stobie followed, leading the extra horses. Stuyve and I brought up the rear.

The cattle were still there on the ice. Simrose, Jimmy John and Aitkens had held them. How those three men, on played-out horses, had been able to keep that herd together and out of the timber for so long a time remains a mystery to this day, both to myself and to the boys who held them there.

AC

Our reinforcements, men and horses, managed the crossing without mishap and it was a comfort to me to have company this time in the cold and plunging water.

"We've got 'em," croaked Simrose, as we rode in close. "Don't think a one's got back on us."

Jimmy John yelled, "Give me a fresh cayuse, turn us loose and let her buck. Nothing too good for a cowboy."

From *Nothing Too Good for a Cowboy*

Born in Washington, DC, Richmond P. Hobson Jr., lived in Alabama, California, New York and east Texas, working at almost everything from insurance salesman to roughneck in the oil fields, always saving to buy a cattle ranch. He lost his savings in the stock market crash and drifted to Wyoming, where he met Panhandle Phillips, who dreamt of building a ranch in northern B.C.

The two were penniless, but found backers and a four-million-acre ranch, which became the Frontier Cattle Company. But five years later war threatened their venture. There were too few men to help with the cattle and there was not enough hay to feed the animals through the winter or money to buy any. Refusing to give up, the partners survived the winter of 1939 with help from their friends and managed to hold on until things began to improve. Hobson has written two other books about his cowboy adventures, *The Grass Beyond the Mountains* and *The Rancher Takes a Wife.*

A Fiery Celebration

by R.B. Townshend
Colorado, about 1875

My Christmas was spent in the cabin of old Horn, the hunter, and on Christmas Day the cabin got on fire, and we spent most of the day in putting it out with a bucket and two tin cups. However, our primitive fire-engine was successful.

The valley is very beautiful, fertile, and well watered. I do not know whether it is marked in the map, but it is the valley immediately north-west of the head of the Huerfano (pronounced Wharfanno). Coming back I took rather a different route; for, by the way I came, I had to ford the Arkansas. This was not pleasant, as the stream was running strong and large pieces of loose ice came rushing down. It was long before I could get my pony to face it, for the moment he got in and the ice struck him he plunged back again, but at last by a vigorous use of the spur I got him through all right.

To avoid this ford, however, I followed an Indian trail down through the mountains on the south bank. I had to walk all the way, as the hills were very steep and the trail narrow. In one place we had to cross a small river which had been flooded and frozen over, but the ice in the middle had broken away so that it could neither be jumped nor forded. At last, I found a narrow bridge of ice right across. So I got sand and sanded it all the way over, and then with some trouble brought the pony over. It was barely a foot wide in the middle, and he did not like it, but there was no other way, as the cañon above and below was impassable.

As we emerged from the hills I found I had dropped a blanket, so I went back for it and on the way I saw two large deer. I hunted them some time but could not get a shot. The buck had the finest horns I have seen. You need not alarm yourself about my solitary journeys, for there are no hostile Indians here, and I always go well armed. I think of returning to the Eastern States for a bit in the spring, but do not know where or when…

From *A Tenderfoot in Colorado*

When young Robert Townshend arrived in the Rockies in 1869, just off the boat from England, he was a greenhorn, at the mercy of every gambler and conman he met. He quickly sought out seasoned cowboys and frontiersmen who taught him how to survive in the Wild West, including such skills as how to cook beans and kill buffalo.

He prospected for gold and started a ranch in Arkansas. Five years later he sold out and returned to England, where he concentrated on golf, tennis and writing.

Son-of-a-Bitch Stew

2	cloves garlic, minced
1 teaspoon	ground cumin
1 teaspoon	salt
1/2 teaspoon	pepper
1/4 teaspoon	cinnamon
1/4 cup	packed brown sugar
5 pounds	boneless beef chuck steak, cut into 1 1/2-inch cubes
2 tablespoons	vegetable oil
2	large onions, cut into wedges
1	green pepper, cut into chunks
12-ounce bottle	dark beer
2	tomatoes diced, or 3 tablespoons tomato paste
1 teaspoon	dried chili flakes
16	peeled baby carrots
10	small new potatoes or 2 pounds potatoes, cubed

Preheat oven to 325°F.

In a small bowl, stir together garlic, cumin, salt, pepper, cinnamon and 1 tablespoon of the brown sugar. Rub over beef and let stand for 1 hour at room temperature.

In a large ovenproof saucepan, heat oil over medium-high heat. In batches, cook meat, turning occasionally, for 5 minutes or until well browned; transfer meat to a bowl. Add onions and green pepper to saucepan; cook 5 minutes or until softened. Return meat to saucepan. Stir in beer, tomato, chili flakes and remaining brown sugar. Cover, put in oven and bake for 2 hours.

Stir in carrots and potatoes, cover and cook 1 to 1 1/2 hours longer or until vegetables and beef are tender. Serves 8 to 10.

From *The Wild West Cookbook*
This stew is the modern equivalent of a traditional chuckwagon meal. Almost any part of the butchered beef might be thrown into the pot, since cowboys don't waste anything edible. Any kind of vegetables can be included. There's a cowboy saying that if you can tell what's in it, it ain't been cooked long enough.

Bear Sign

by Andy Adams
North Platte, Nebraska, 1882

Cowboy John Officer relates a Christmas memory:

Well, three days before Christmas, just when things were looking gloomiest, there drifted up from the Cheyenne country one of the old timers. None of them had seen him in four years, though he had worked on that range before, and with the exception of myself, they all knew him. He was riding the chuckline all right, but Miller gave him a welcome, as he was the real thing. He had been working out in the Pan-handle country, New Mexico, and the devil knows where, since he had left that range. He was meaty with news and scarey stories. The boys would sit around and listen to him yarn, and now and then a smile would come on their faces. Miller was delighted with his guest. He had shown no signs of letting up at eleven o'clock the first night, when he happened to mention where he was the Christmas before.

"'There was a little woman at the ranch,' said he, 'wife of the owner, and I was helping her get up dinner, as we had quite a number of folks at the ranch. She asked me to make the bear sign—doughnuts, she called them—and I did, though she had to show me how some little. Well, fellows, you ought to have seen them—just sweet enough, browned to a turn, and enough to last a week. All the folks at dinner that day praised them. Since then, I've had a chance to try my hand several times, and you may not tumble to the diversity of all my accomplishments, but I'm an artist on bear sign.'

"Miller arose, took him by the hand, and said, 'That's straight, now, is it?'

"'That's straight. Making bear sign is my long suit.'

"'Mouse,' said Miller to one of the boys, 'go out and bring in his saddle from the stable and put it under my bed. Throw his horse in the big pasture in the morning. He stays here until spring; and the first spear of green grass I see, his name goes on the pay roll. This outfit is shy on men who can make bear sign. Now, I was thinking that you could spread down your blankets on the hearth, but you can sleep with me to-night. You go to work on this specialty of yours right after breakfast in the morning, and show us what you can do in that line.'

"They talked quite a while longer, and then turned in for the night. The next morning after breakfast was over, he got the needed articles together and went to work. But there was a surprise in store for him. There was nearly a dozen men lying around, all able eaters. By ten o'clock he began to turn them out as he said he could. When the regular cook had to have the stove to get dinner, the taste which we had had made us ravenous for more. Dinner over, he went at them again in earnest. A boy riding towards the railroad with an important letter dropped in, and as he claimed he could only stop for a moment, we stood aside until he had had a taste, though he filled himself like a poisoned pup. After eating a solid hour, he filled his pockets and rode away. One of our regular men called after him, 'Don't tell anybody what we got.'

"We didn't get any supper that night. Not a man could have eaten a bite. Miller made him knock off along in the shank of the evening, as he had done enough for any one day. The next morning after breakfast he fell to at the bear sign once more. Miller rolled a barrel of flour into the kitchen from the storehouse, and told him to fly at them. 'About how many do you think you'll want?' asked our bear sign man.

"'That big tub full won't be any too many,' answered Miller. 'Some of these fellows haven't had any of this kind of truck since they were little boys. If this gets out, I look for men from other camps.'

"'The fellow fell to his work like a thoroughbred, which he surely was. About ten o'clock two men rode up from a camp to the north, which the boy had passed the day before with the letter. They never went near the dug-out, but straight to the kitchen. That movement showed that they were on to the racket. An hour later old Tom Cave rode in, his horse all in a lather, all the way from Garretson's camp, twenty-five miles to the east. The old sinner said that he had been on the frontier some little time, and that they were the best bear sign he had tasted in forty years. He refused to take a stool and sit down like civilized folks, but stood up by the tub and picked out the ones which were a pale brown.

"After dinner our man threw off his overshirt, unbuttoned his red undershirt and turned it in until you could see the hair on his breast. Rolling up his sleeves, he flew at his job once more. He was getting his work reduced to a science by this time. He rolled his dough, cut his dough, and turned out the fine brown bear sign to the satisfaction of all.

"His capacity, however, was limited. About two o'clock Doc Langford and two of his peelers were seen riding up. When he came into the kitchen, Doc swore by all that was good and holy that he hadn't heard that our artist had come back to that country. But any one that was noticing could see him edge around to the tub. It was easy to see that he was lying. This luck of ours was circulating faster than a secret amongst women. Our man, though, stood at his post like the boy on the burning deck. When night came on, he hadn't covered the bottom of the tub. When he knocked off, Doc Langford and his men gobbled up what was left. We gave them a mean look as they rode off, but they came back the next day, five strong. Our regular men around camp didn't like it, the way things were going. They tried to act polite to—"

"Calling bear signs doughnuts," interrupted Quince Forrest, "reminds me of what—"

"Will you kindly hobble your lips," said Officer; "I have the floor at present. As I was saying, they tried to act polite to company that way, but we hadn't got a smell the second day. Our man showed no signs of fatigue, and told several good stories that night. He was tough. The next day was Christmas, but he showed no respect for a holiday, and made up a large batch of dough before breakfast. It was a good thing he did, for early that morning 'Original' John Smith and four of his peelers rode in from the west, their horses all covered with frost. They must have started at daybreak—it was a good twenty-two-mile ride. They wanted us to believe that they had simply come over to spend Christmas with us. Company that way, you can't say anything. But the easy manner in which they gravitated around that tub— not even waiting to be invited—told a different tale. They were not nearly satisfied by noon.

"Then who should come drifting in as we were sitting down to dinner, but Billy Dunlap and Jim Hale from Quinlan's camp, thirty miles south on the Cimarron. Dunlap always holed up like a bear in the winter, and several of the boys spilled their coffee at the sight of him. He put up a thin excuse just like the rest. Any one could see through it. But there it was again—he was company. Lots of us had eaten at his camp and complained of his chuck; therefore, we were nice to him. Miller called our man out from behind the kitchen and told him to knock off if he wanted to. But he wouldn't do it. He was clean strain—I'm not talking. Dunlap ate hardly any dinner, we noticed, and the very first batch of bear sign turned out, he loads up a tin plate and goes out and sits behind the storehouse in the sun, all alone in his glory. He satisfied himself out of the tub after that."

From *The Log of a Cowboy*
A narrative of the old trail days
Andy Adams is considered one of the most authentic writers about Western life. Born in Indiana in 1859, he was only a boy when he left home to become a cowboy. For fifteen years he rode the cattle trails, and his reminiscences of those rides from Texas to Montana tell what a cowboy's life in those days was really like.

He left cowboying in 1890 and tried his hand at many things, before settling down to write about his experiences on the trail. *The Log of a Cowboy,* written in 1903, was his first book. Though followed by many others, it remained his most popular.

Christmas Greeting

by Tom Mix
Christmas, 1926

A Proclamation

We, your true friends, by virtue of the love and affection vested in sincere friendship, do hereby prescribe and proclaim a day of cheer, a year of joy to you and yours, at this Yule time and at the birth of this New Year of our Lord, one thousand nine hundred and twenty six.

Tom Mix, Victoria Mix
and Thomasina Mix

Cowboy movie star Tom Mix was born in 1880 in Pennsylvania. He served in the Spanish-American War and later moved to Oklahoma, where he was a ranch hand, bartender and, for a brief time, marshal in Dewey, Oklahoma. He began making movies in 1909, and in all made 336 feature films, produced 88, wrote 71 and directed 117.

Mix was an amazing athlete. He and his horse Tony performed all their own stunts.

Harking Back

by Charles A. Siringo
Texas, about 1900

I arrived in Amarillo, Texas, at three o'clock Christmas morning. A blizzard was raging and the weather was very cold. Knowing that my old cowboy friend of early days, Jack Ryan, kept a saloon in this town, I concluded to go there and warm up. On entering Ryan's place I found Jack behind the bar.

After shaking hands, Jack asked if I could recognize any of my old friends among the drunken men sleeping on the floor, chairs and tables. Casting my eyes over the bunch I picked out my friend Burkley Howe sleeping in a chair and dead to the world from overindulgence in "firewater." In looking at him my mind drifted back to 1878, when he, then a fine looking, sober young man of high education and wealthy parents, came to the Panhandle of Texas, then a wild, unsettled country, to learn the cattle business. He came from Massachusetts, the former home of David T. Beals, Erskine Clement and Mr. Bates, for whom I was then employed. As I was then boss of an outfit on the staked plains where the little city of Amarillo now stands, Howe was turned over to me to be taught the cattle business.

Now, here sat that same Burkley Howe on this Christmas morning, over twenty years later, a total wreck and aged beyond his years from that greatest of all evils, liquor.

Slapping him on the shoulder I said: "Hello there, Burkley Howe, old boy!"

Before opening his eyes he yelled: "Well, I'll be d—d if there isn't Charlie Siringo!" He had recognized my voice. He then jumped up and began hugging me and declaring to the other drunken men who had awakened when he yelled that I used to be the best wild-horse rider in the United States. He had seen me ride some "bad" horses and he couldn't brag on me enough. In order to choke him off, I called the crowd to take up a Christmas drink with me.

Ryan then informed me that my old friend, John Hollicott, the manager of the L X ranch, which I had helped establish, was at a saloon across the street celebrating Christmas. Running across the street I found Hollicott dancing a jig and having a rattling good time, as he called it. He almost choked me as he dragged me up to the bar to take a Christmas drink "on him." The whole crowd of a dozen men were called up to drink. I was the hero of the moment with Hollicott. Finally we went across to Jack Ryan's place and Howe joined in the celebration.

At daylight Hollicott's coachman hitched up the spirited team of mules and we started for the L X ranch on the Canadian river twenty miles north, to take Christmas dinner with the "boys" and girls there.

I left poor Howe laid out on the floor and I haven't seen him since, but I was informed through friends that he died a year or two later which proves what liquor can do in a twenty years' tussle with robust manhood.

We had a cold ride against the raging blizzard with the thermometer ten degrees below zero, hence the cork was pulled from the five-gallon jug several times before reaching the ranch.

It was about 10 a.m. when we reached the roaring fire in the large stone fireplace which I had helped to build over twenty years before. There was the identical hearthstone put in place by W.C. Moore, the outlaw murderer whom I met in Juneau, Alaska, and me.

Thoughts of bygone days flew thick and fast, and the flames from the log fire seemed to be playing hide and seek with other bright blazes of long ago. Possibly my familiarity with the jug en route from Amarillo had something to do with my imagination.

Hollicott introduced me to the Lee family who lived on the ranch. The head of the household was Mr. Garnett Lee, then came his good-looking, black-eyed wife and their two beautiful young lady daughters. The younger, a girl of eighteen, had just come from a college in middle Texas to spend the holidays. She was indeed a little "peach," and it was all I could do to keep from falling in love with her, even though I was old enough to be her father.

Several of Hollicott's cowboys from outside camps were on hand to sample the Christmas dinner. Two of them, Charlie Sprague and Johnny Bell, were former chums of mine and had worked under me when I was a "boss" on this ranch. The others I had never met before.

About 2 p.m. the fat gobbler and cranberry sauce, with the side "fixens" were set on the same old table from which the noted outlaw "Billy the Kid" and I ate meals together twenty years previous. It was a dinner fit for kings and queens, and we all did justice to it. When we got through Mr. Turkey-gobbler looked as though he had been to a bone-picking match.

The afternoon was spent "harking back" and sampling the contents of the jug.

At night, after supper, one of the boys got out his violin and the dance started. There being only three ladies present we had to make a girl out of one of the "boys" by tying a handkerchief around his arm, in order to fill out the set.

Towards morning the jug began to work on Hollicott and he wouldn't let me dance. He insisted on "harking back" to the early days of our cowboy lives. He and I first met in 1876 in Kiowa, Kansas, at which time he was a cowboy for the Hunter & Evans cattle outfit, and I was drifting around to give my mustache a chance to grow.[…]

Towards daylight the dance broke up and the coachman drove Hollicott and me to our Christmas "jag" up to the mouth of Pitcher Creek, a couple of miles, where Hollicott had his private home.

From *A Cowboy Detective*

Charles Siringo was first and foremost a cowboy. He owned a ranch in Sante Fe, New Mexico and even though his work as a sleuth for the Pinkerton National Detective Agency took him to many places in North America—including Alaska, British Columbia and Old Mexico—he always returned to his ranch. He worked as a cowboy detective for twenty-two years, tracking outlaws and rustlers, swindlers and con men. Siringo died in 1928, aged seventy-two.

Three Wise Men

by S. Omar Barker

Back in the days when cattle range was prairies wide and lone,
Three Bar Z hands was winter-camped upon the Cimarrón.
Their callin' names was Booger Bill and Pinto Pete and Tug,
And though their little dugout camp was plenty warm and snug,
They got plumb discontented, for with Christmas drawin' near,
They couldn't see no prospects of no kind of Christmas cheer.

Pete spoke about the bailes he'd be missin' up at Taos.
Tug said he'd give his gizzard just to see a human house
Alight with Christmas candles; and ol' Booger Bill avowed
He'd shoot the next galoot who spoke of Christmas cheer out loud.
They sure did have the lonesomes, but the first of Christmas week,
A wagonload of immigrants made camp off down the creek.

They'd come out from Missouri and was headin' farther west,
But had to stop a little while and give their team a rest.
They seemed to be pore nester folks, with maybe six or eight
As hungry lookin', barefoot kids as ever licked a plate.
"We've just got beans to offer you," the wagon woman smiled,
"But if you boys will join us, I will have a big pot b'iled
On Christmas day for dinner, and we'll do the best we kin
To make it seem like Christmas time, although our plates are tin!"

Them cowboys sort of stammered, but they promised her they'd come,
Then loped back to their dugout camp, and things began to hum.
They whittled with their pocketknives, they sewed with rawhide
      threads,
They hammered and they braided and they raveled rope to shreds.
They butchered out a yearlin', and they baked a big ol' roast.
They scratched their heads to figger out what kids would like the most,

Till when they went on Christmas day to share the nesters' chuck,
They had a packhorse loaded with their homemade Christmas truck:
Bandanna dolls for little gals, with raveled rope for hair;
Some whittled wooden guns for boys, and for each kid a pair
Of rough-made rawhide moccasins. You should have seen the look
Upon the nester woman's face when from their pack they took
A batch of pies plumb full of prunes, some taffy made of lick,
And a pan of sourdough biscuits right around four inches thick.

That ain't the total tally, but it sort of gives a view
Of what three lonesome cowboys figgered out to try and do
To cure the Christmas lonesomes on the Cimarrón, amid
The wild coyotes and cattle—and they found it sure 'nough did!

From *Rawhide Rhymes*
In his prolific and distinguished
writing career, S. Omar Barker wrote
more than 1200 articles, 1500 short
stories and about 2500 poems. He
knew the cowboy's life firsthand, as
he was born and raised on his parents'
mountain homestead in New Mexico,
and never strayed very far from home,
except to serve in France during the
First World War.

Boots

by Will James

The winter went on mighty peaceful and without any events out of the ordinary happening, not excepting maybe one, one that was a great surprise and pleasure to me. A rider had come by our camp and left a package and when he'd rode on, I was right on the job watching Bopy open that package. A cardboard box was unwrapped. He handed it to me and said, as he'd said more times afterwards:

"C'est pour toi, Billee. Bonne et heureuse nouvelle anneé." (It's for you, Billy. Good and happy New Year.)

I don't think I hardly heard him as I took the cover off that box and looked inside. There, all shining, was the copper toes of a little pair of boots. Part of the top was red and a star was designed in the center of that.

That was my first New Year's present from Bopy, and whenever he was where he could get me a present he'd always pick on New Year's day to give it to me, for according to his bringing up, that was the big day for cheer and to celebrate and give presents on. Christmas was a day for quiet and peace. All he'd do on Christmas day was to spread out the best meal he could and he was sure a bear at doing that.

From *Lone Cowboy*

Will James was born in 1892 in Quebec, Canada. By the age of four he was drawing on the kitchen floor. He drifted to the United States while a teenager and worked at many jobs before he began to sell his sketches.

In 1922 he sold his first story, "Bucking Horse Riders." His fictional autobiography, *Lone Cowboy*, was written in 1930. He wrote and illustrated twenty-three books, several of which were made into movies. He died in 1942.

Braised Wild Boar with Roasted Pepper Honey Whiskey Sauce

by Chef Goettler at Normand's Restaurant

2 whole	red peppers roasted, then diced
4 ounces	whiskey
3 ounces	liquid honey
1 tablespoon	black pepper (coarse)
1 tablespoon	seasoning salt
6 cups	brown sauce "demi glaze"
8	wild boar loin chops

Mix all ingredients (except chops) well. Pour into a pot with chops. Cover. Braise in oven for 3 to 3 1/2 hours at 350°F. Remove chops from broth. Reduce broth, season to taste. Pour broth over chops and serve. Very easy! and very tasty!

If wild boar is hard to come by in your area, try this recipe with pork chops.

Dynamite

by C.E. MacConnell
Perico, Texas, 1909

Several men from down below had been sent up to Farwell Park to help with the Kaffir corn job and so there was more than the usual activity around the camp. Since Christmas was close at hand they had pooled their money and sent ten dollars up to the Texas Club at Texline for two gallons of I.W. Harper. These came down to Perico in two cartons of four quarts each which were brought to the Park on the saddle horns of a couple of riders.

One of the cartons was opened, a quart taken out, and uncapped, and its contents soon filled the extended glasses of expectant cowboys. The camp began to take on the air of celebration. Bill Lytle, a six-foot-two-inch, two-hundred-twenty-pound cowboy, began to feel especially good after he found a bottle of peroxide on the window sill from which he took a swig and, foaming at the mouth like a mad coyote, let out yells of laughter in which he was joined by most of the crew.

He started to sit down on one end of the wash bench but his weight was too far out on the end and the bench tipped up, scattering the wash basin, bucket and soap. Bill landed upon his back with the bench standing on end between his legs. This seemed to strike him as very funny and he started to rake his spurs over the bench and, between peals of laughter, yell like he was riding a bronc.

Tiring of his amusement after a while, Bill calmed down somewhat and came over to sit on the end of my bed as he inquired about my health. By then the rest inside the house and out of the direct rays of the sun had brought my sight back all right although the touch of dysentery still lingered.

Normally Bill was affable and congenial, sort of happy-go-lucky, but when he had been drinking he was wholly unpredictable, and always dangerous. He was an expert with a rifle or six-gun and never a man to trifle with.[…]

Rufe had a number of colorful calendar pictures of beautiful women pinned up on the walls of the room and these soon attracted Bill's attention. Taking Rufe's .22 caliber rifle which stood in the corner, Bill said he thought he could improve them and began shooting holes into them in the most obvious places. This seemed to give him great pleasure but I hoped he would soon become bored and I tried hard to talk him into putting up the gun.

Finally he quit and, getting up, walked to the end of the bed while he smilingly argued with me. His attention seemed to be centering on the ornate rosettes sewed to my arm bands. My discomfort increased as he slowly raised the rifle and took aim. With amusing comments he carefully shot off both the rosettes and, laughing loudly, put up the gun and went out.

Through the acrid smell of the gun smoke came a whiff of cold air as one of the boys opened the door in answer to a hail from the outside. It was Larry Kehoe, the section boss at Perico, coming to bring holiday greetings to his friends, the cowboys. He was all bright smiles and cheery platitudes but made no mention of the fact that he had seen the trainmen unload two cartons at the station which looked like they might contain liquor and which were later picked up by the cowboys.

It didn't take a conference for the cowboys to figure out the reason for the call and they decided to have some fun with Larry. Although the opened bottle stood in plain sight on the kitchen table almost at his elbow, nobody offered Larry a drink despite his frequent glances at it as he sat at the table. Larry made himself as entertaining as possible by telling some of his rich Irish stories and everyone wondered how long he could stand the strain before breaking down and asking for a drink. He held out for quite a while but finally one of the boys said, "Larry, how would you like a little drink?"

"Don't care if I do." And without further delay he filled a drinking glass full which he set on the table in front of him. Taking out a toothpick, he dipped it into the liquor and savored its quality by solemn shakes of the head, pleased smiles and complimentary remarks.

"Hmm, that's good," he said, licking his lips and relishing the aroma.

We all watched with interest as he finally picked up the glass. Pop-eyed, we saw him drink that glass full of concentrated dynamite as though it were only water. There were, of course, the usual salty comments which follow such a demonstration, and then curiosity got the best of one of the boys who solicitously inquired if Larry didn't think he had better balance that one with one for the other wing.

"Well, now, don't care if I do. But then I'll have to get back to the section. My wife will be lookin' for me." And he filled his glass again.

This one followed the other in the same manner, and we began to wonder what in the world was holding the fellow up since liquor seemed to have no effect upon him. He sat there chatting happily along with no outward evidence of having had even one drink. There was no perceptible difference in his bearing, he didn't slur his words and his laughter was at no higher pitch.

Not many cowboys were teetotalers but a drinking glass of straight liquor is a man-sized drink in any man's language, and here was this little fellow putting away two of them as though they were water from a spring. We wondered if his pipes were lined with brass, and just what was his capacity.

"Well, I'll have to go now for sure. They will be missing me at the station." But he made no move to get up.

"Hell, Larry, you better split them two down the middle. After all, Christmas comes only once a year."

"That's right nice of you. Many thanks for the hospitality and a Merry Christmas." And a third tumblerful followed the other two. Larry stood up, repeated his Christmas greetings, expressed his many thanks, took one step and fell flat on his face, dead to the world.

As long as he sat still the liquor left him alone but the minute he moved it hit him a KO.

We saddled a horse, loaded Larry across the saddle like a sack of wheat and led the horse down to the section house. Maria, Larry's wife, came running out, sized up the situation, blistered us with invective for treating Larry like that and, gathering him up in her arms, carried him into the house.

From *XIT Buck*

Charles E. MacConnell, nicknamed Buck, left home at thirteen and wandered around the West, working at whatever he could. He ended up at a ranch in New Mexico Territory and within a few years was a skilled bronco buster. He settled at the XIT, the largest ranch in Texas. His story is one of the Old West, gunfights, rowdy brawls, trail drives and rustlers.

The Cowboys' Christmas Ball

by Larry Chittenden
Anson, Texas, 1891

Way out in Western Texas, where the Clear Fork's waters flow,
Where the cattle are a-browsin' and the Spanish Ponies grow;
Where the Northers come a-whistlin' from beyond the Neutral Strip;
And the prairie dogs are sneezin', as though they had the grip;
Where the coyotes come a-howlin' round the ranches after dark,
And the mockin' birds are singin' to the lovely medder lark;
Where the 'possum and the badger and the rattlesnakes abound,
And the monstrous stars are winkin' o'er a wilderness profound;
Where lonesome, tawny prairies melt into airy streams,
While the Double Mountains slumber in heavenly kinds of dreams;
Where the antelope is grazin' and the lonely plovers call,
It was there I attended the Cowboys' Christmas Ball.

The town was Anson City, old Jones' county seat,
Where they raised Polled Angus cattle and waving whiskered wheat;
Where the air is soft and bammy and dry and full of health,
Where the prairies is explodin' with agricultural wealth;
Where they print the Texas Western, that Hall McCann supplies
With news and yarns and stories, of most amazin' size;
Where Frank Smith "pulls the badger" on knowin' tenderfeet,
And Democracy's triumphant and mighty hard to beat;
Where lives that good old hunter, John Milsap, from Lamar,
Who used to be sheriff "back east in Paris, sah."
'Twas there, I say, at Anson with the lovely Widder Wall,
That I went to that reception, The Cowboys' Christmas Ball.

The boys had left the ranches and come to town in piles;
The ladies, kinder scatterin', had gathered in for miles.
And yet the place was crowded, as I remember well,
'Twas gave on this occasion at the Morning Star Hotel.
The music was a fiddle and a lively tambourine,
And viol came imported, by the stage from Abilene.
The room was togged out gorgeous—with mistletoe and shawls,
And the candles flickered festious, around the airy walls.
The wimmen folks looked lovely—the boys looked kinder treed,
Till the leader commenced yellin', "Whoa, fellers, let's stampede,"
And the music started sighin' and a-wailin' through the hall
As a kind of introduction to the Cowboys' Christmas Ball.

The leader was a feller that came from Thompson's ranch,
They called him Windy Billy from Little Deadman's Branch.
His rig was kinder keerless, big spurs and high-heeled boots;
He had a reputation that comes when fellers shoots.
His voice was like a bugle upon the mountain height;
His feet were animated and a mighty movin' sight,
When he commenced to holler, "Now, fellers stake your pen.
Lock horns ter all them heifers and rustle them like men;
Saloot yer lovely critters; now swing and let 'em go;
Climb the grapevine round 'em; now all hands do-ce-do.
You maverick, jine the round-up, jess skip the waterfall,"
Huh, hit was gettin' active, the Cowboys' Christmas Ball.

The boys was tol'able skittish, the ladies powerful neat;
The old brass viol's music just got there with both feet;
That wailin' frisky fiddle, I never shall forget;
And Windy kept a-singin'—I think I hear him yet—
"Oh yes, chase yer squirrels and cut 'em to our side;
Spur Treadwell to the center, with Cross P Charley's bride;
Doc Hollis down the center, and twine the ladies' chain;
Van Andrews, pen the fillies in big T Diamond's train.
All pull your freight together, now swallow fork and change;
Big Boston, lead the trail herd through little Pitchfork's range.
Purr round yer gentle [kitties], now rope and balance all."
Huh, hit were gettin' active—the Cowboys' Christmas Ball.

The dust riz fast and furious; we all jes' galloped round,
Till the scenery got so giddy that T Bar Dick was downed.
We buckled to our pardners and told 'em to hold on,
Then shook our hoofs like lightnin' until the early dawn.
Don't tell me 'bout cotillions, or germans—no, sir-ee!
That whirl at Anson City jes' takes the cake with me.
I'm sick of lazy shufflin's, of them I've had my fill;
Give me a frontier break-down backed by Windy Bill.
McAllister ain't nowhere, when Windy leads the show;
I've seen 'em both in harness, and so I ought ter know.
Oh, Bill, I shan't forget yer, and I oftentimes recall
That lively gaited sworray—the Cowboys' Christmas Ball.

From *Songs of the Cowboys*

About 1885, Larry Chittenden came to Texas from New Jersey, where he was a reporter for the *New York Times*. He fell in love with the place and eventually bought a ranch.

Several years later, in 1891, he composed this classic poem, which has become a Christmas tradition at dances and plays throughout Texas. Chittenden died in 1934, the same year that the citizens of Anson decided to make the Cowboys' Christmas Ball an annual event.

Wind and Weasels

by Andy Russell
Alberta, early 1900s

When the temperatures were well below zero with a north wind adding to the chill riding anywhere was an exercise in endurance. One of us would always ride the fourteen miles to town on Christmas Eve to get the mail and whatever odds and ends of groceries that mother wanted. I made one ride when it was twenty-odd degrees below zero straight into the teeth of a nasty north wind. It was so cold that I had to get off my horse and walk ahead of him—not easy with all the clothes I had on plus Dad's woolskin chaps. My saddle, like most of them, had a hole under its fork below the horn and, chaps designed as they are, the wind whistled through, chilling my crotch. I finally got so numb with cold that I stopped at a ranch belonging to a French Canadian to warm up. He had a numerous family, including a daughter about my age, and when I came in the door the good lady of the house, surrounded by kids, was all smiles as she helped me off with my coat. About that time the daughter put a big mug of hot cocoa on the kitchen table which I gratefully sipped while feeling the warmth spread out all through me. Suddenly I became aware of thawing out, for a painful burning sensation assailed me in a very private part of my anatomy. It was pure agony and I stood up from the table to stamp around in a sort of wild dance with my face tied in a knot.

Winter woollies (NA2390-6)

"Must be chilblains," I gasped. "It'll be all right in a minute."

As soon as possible I escaped through the door, thanking the lady, and, wishing them all a Merry Christmas, got back on my horse and headed for town.

After I had tied my horse in a stall at the livery stable, I sneaked a look at my still throbbing appendage. It was so tender I could scarcely stand to touch it. As I looked after my errands, I worried it would drop off like calves' tails sometimes did when they froze. The trip back home was made in record time and was much warmer with the wind in my back. For a few days I was very careful when moving around, but kept my misfortune to myself. Urinating was very painful for a while. In due course I healed up, but knowing I would be very sensitive to cold I made some preparations for another hard day in the saddle, should it come.

Through some talk or reading I had done, I knew the old Indians protected themselves on cold rides by making a sheath from a weasel skin and tying it with a cord around their waists. So I picked a suitable skin out of the collection taken on my trapline and proceeded to tan it. For the rest of the winter I wore it with the fur in against my skin all the time. Come spring I hung it up in the back of my clothes closet, where my mother found it while cleaning house.

"What on earth is this?" she asked me.

So I told her and she handed it back to me as she shook her head and left looking somewhat amazed. When my father heard about it, he roared with laughter. He also told me that some of the old cowboys had used such a contraption in winter.

From *The Canadian Cowboy: Stories of Cows, Cowboys, and Cayuses*
Canada's premier cowboy, Andy Russell, grew up on his family's ranch. His grandfather was one of the early ranchers in Alberta. Russell, who has worked as an outfitter, a guide and even a bronco buster, is renowned for his books and short stories of his adventurous life in the Rocky Mountains and the Canadian West.

I Am a Busted Cowboy

by Iyam B. Usted
Montana, 1893

I am a busted cowboy
And I work upon the range;
In summertime I get some work
But one thing that is strange,
As soon as Fall work's over
We get it in the neck
And we get a Christmas present
On a neatly written check.
Then come to town to rusticate,
We've no place else to stay
When Winter winds are howling
Because we can't eat hay.
A puncher's life's a picnic;
It's one continued joke,
But there's none more anxious to see Spring
Than a cowboy who is broke.
The wages that a cowboy earns
In Summer go like smoke,
And when the Winter snows have come
You bet your life he's broke.

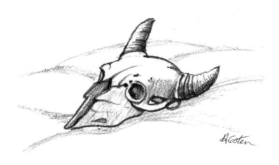

You can talk about your Holiday,
Your Christmas cheer and joy;
It's all the same to me, my friend,
Cash gone—I'm a broke cowboy.
My saddle and my gun's in soak;
My spurs I've long since sold;
My rawhide and my quirt are gone;
My chaps—no, they're too old;
My stuff's all gone, I can't even beg
A solitary smoke,
For no one cares what becomes of
A cowboy who is broke.
Now where I'll eat my dinner
This Christmas, I don' know,
But you bet I'm going to have one
If they give me half a show.
This Christmas has no charms for me;
On good things I'll not choke,
Unless I get a big hand-out—
I'm a cowboy who is broke.

 From *Stock Growers' Journal,*
Miles City, Montana in their
December 1893 issue

All Kinds of Bad Weather

by Will Tom Carpenter
Alpine, Texas, 1892

The fall of 1892 during Xmas week, I pulled out with about 1,760 head. We had all Kinds of bad weather during the time we was gathering those cattle. It was about 10 miles south of Alpine in the mountains, and it was trying to storm and do Everything Else but something nice. The fog would be so thick of nights that we couldn't see the cattle, and they would just walk off from 7 or 8 men on gard. We lost the herd 3 different nights before we got off with them. You see it was right in their Range and they wanted to get away and did.

At the wind-up it snowed and cleared off, leaving about 2 1/2 inches of snow on the ground. It was pretty cold sailing. We crossed the S-P-R-R[1] about 4 miles east of Alpine, Xmas Eve. Ft. Stockton was on the route, a distance of about 40 miles, if I am not mistaken. When we got within about 12 miles of Stockton, one Evening pretty late, it began to rain and in a short time the rain turned to snow, so we struck Camp. We had two wagons, one being a Corn wagon, for we had to feed our horses. We beded the herd up against the south side of a Hill, called the 12 mile Hill. It wasn't much of a wind break, but it was the best in sight.

[1] The Southern Pacific Railroad.

Those cattle walked & troted until three O'Clock in the morning. They would walk up hill & trot down hill. We all was around the herd, and there was plenty of sotol² so we built fires all around the herd. Guess we must of had as many as a dozen fires or more, and we would leave our horses standing at the fires and take it afoot. About 3 O'Clock in the morning it quit snowing & went to freezing, then the cattle layed down. I sent all of the men to the wagon to go to bed but myself and another man.

The next morning we left 6 head of Cattle on the bed ground, being too near dead to get up. But oh, suffering snakes, wasn't it cold!

From *Lucky 7: A Cowman's Autobiography*
The youngest of seven children, Will Carpenter was born in 1854 in Missouri. With his family he moved to Kansas and then to Texas with his brother in 1872. Despite his family's efforts to teach him "book learning," he attended school for only part of three sessions, preferring the open spaces. He rode the cattle drives of Texas, Oklahoma, New Mexico, Kansas, Colorado, Nevada, Utah and Arizona as a cowboy and trail boss.

He retired to his own ranch in Pecos in 1900, saddened by the changes to the open prairies as fences were erected and vast ranches divided.

---

²A palmlike cactus that usually grows to six or seven feet in height and about one and a half feet in trunk diameter. The long, narrow leaves remain on the trunk after they die and make a roaring blaze when the trunk is set on fire.

Prairie Oysters

1 pound	calf testicles (about 24)
2	eggs
1/4 cup	milk
1 cup	cornmeal
1/2 cup	flour
1/2 cup	finely crushed soda crackers (about 14 crackers)
1 teaspoon	salt
1/4 teaspoon	freshly ground black pepper
1/4 teaspoon	cayenne pepper to taste
	canola oil for frying

Butterfly the oysters by slicing open lengthwise without cutting completely in half. Peel off outer membrane. Cover with salted water and soak overnight in refrigerator.

In a bowl, beat eggs and milk until frothy. In a separate bowl, stir together cornmeal, flour, cracker crumbs, salt, pepper and cayenne pepper.

In a large cast-iron skillet, heat about 1/2 inch of canola oil over medium-high heat. Drain oysters. In batches, dip in beaten egg mixture, roll in cornmeal mixture and fry in hot oil 5 minutes, turning halfway, or until golden brown and cooked through. Serve hot.

From *The Wild West Cookbook*
Prairie oysters must be eaten fresh, says Cinda Chavich, the cookbook's author, and therefore will never really be eaten at Christmas. Prairie oysters (or mountain oysters, as they're also known) are a traditional treat during spring branding, when male calves are castrated. The tender organ meat is the size of a large chicken liver and actually tastes a little like chicken livers. Testicles from grown bulls are much larger and must be sliced to 1/4 inch thickness before cooking.

Peeling the smaller calf testicles is time-consuming but important, unless you like your oysters chewy!

Cattle Christmas

by Hank Law
Chilcotin, B.C., early 1900s

Christmas came up fast after the first frost. On the morning of the 25th I fed everything at the barn, hooked my team to a cutter and headed up to the meadows. The temperature was around 40 below zero. The sun was up and the sky was as clear as a light blue crystal dome. The old vetched biddies I was feeding were cold standing around in their skins on a bunch of hard old feet. They looked like a flock of short legged camels with their backs humped that way, but big hearted me, I would fix everything. Yessir! I'd give 'em the feed of their lives. It's Christmas, ain't it? I drove up to the waiting cattle and stood up and bowed, wishing them all a very happy Christmas. Next thing, instead of loading up three loads of hay and scattering it over hell's half acre, I hooked onto the stockyard fence and pulled it down. That was all I had to do. Them old she cows headed in there like a bunch of women going in to a sale, the only difference being when one fell down the others tried not to walk all over her.

The team were interested in something coming over the meadow towards us. I threw a benevolent look in that direction and what met my eyes changed my whole outlook. Because… so help me, with all the teeming millions in the world…there were just two people that shouldn't be there. But there they were, staring at me over that sea of steaming backs. It was the boss and his wife coming to help me with the chores.

The boss's first question gave me my answer. "Wassa matter, they break in on ya? Well," he added, "may as well leave 'em in now,

Even on Christmas day, the cows come home for dinner.

stack's about through anyway. Let's get crackin' at the Christmas turkey." Two hours later we were sitting down to a real feast.

It was great while it lasted but cows have to eat and drink and most of the cowboys attending had a long ride ahead of them. I have often wondered if the people who sit down to a feed of steak ever think of the men who made that steak possible. There have been films on the subject by the thousand. Thousands of books have been written but very, very few tell of the hardships and grief and the eternal battle with the elements that these men of the frontier country endure. At the time these events took place beef was three quarters of a cent a pound on the hoof, perhaps $5 for a prime steer, with a drive across country, up to 200 miles in some cases before reaching the railroad.

From *Chilcotin: Preserving Pioneer Memories*
This collection of stories, by pioneer ranchers who settled the Chilcotin, includes family histories, adventures and some humorous insights into the hardships of early day ranching life.

Stage Fright

by Roy Rogers
Duck Run, Ohio, 1920s

I liked farming and it kept me plenty busy, but I had other interests, too. I played the clarinet a little; I liked sports, especially baseball, and for a while there, I thought I might have a future as a pitcher. Because he thought it would help me get over my shyness, Guy Baumgartner encouraged me to try out for the school play. To my horror and dismay I was cast as Santa Claus, which meant I had to stand up in front of a crowd of people patting my padded belly and saying, "Ho, ho, ho!" As if that weren't bad enough, I then had to sing a little song about Santa heaping the stockings high and carrying toys in a sack on his back. You would have thought I had to deliver a Shakespearean speech, I was so terrified with stage fright. My knees knocked, my teeth chattered, and my mind went blank with panic trying to remember what I was supposed to say. I guess I did manage to croak out the words and the tune and made it through the play, but if anyone told me back then that I would make my fame and fortune as an actor I would have laughed out loud. Nothing could have seemed less likely.

Christmas at home with the family was a wonderful time. We didn't have much money for presents, so I whittled little things out of wood for my sisters and my folks. I made whistles and little boxes for their knickknacks, and we all got together to make ornaments for the tree out of paper and cardboard and strings laced through popcorn and cranberries. We found our tree in the woods out back of our house, and I went out and killed a chicken (Dad never could do that), which Mom cooked up with vegetables she had put up during the fall.

From *Happy Trails: Our Life Story*
The King of the Cowboys, Roy Rogers began his show business career as a singing and yodeling cowboy with his band, Sons of the Pioneers. He shot to fame with his first film in 1938. Later he married his co-star, Dale Evans, and as the King and Queen of the Cowboys, they became legends.

Christmas Horses

Memories of Sarah Parker
Okanagan, B.C., early 1900s

In Christmas time, in winter, the horses stay over here. That's where Harry was raised. When Christmas comes we have church every midnight. Ol' Bercie and Johnny Harris they come over here and stay with us. They put horses in the barn.

Ol' Bercie was fiddle player. He played violin and people started dancing. They dance until about eleven o'clock, then they quit and go to Six Mile Church, on the sleighs. That church would be full of people and we sing Christmas hymns. We all pray and after that we go back to the house again. We start dancing again. The violin player would play again. Ol' Lesime McDougall would call and we dance and dance and dance all night.

From *Stories and Images about what the horse has done for us*
This collection of reminiscences from Elders and community members of the Okanagan Nation is an invaluable record of stories and photographs from the turn of the century and later.

My Cowboy's Night Before Christmas

by David Kelley

'Twas just before Santy came,
the story is told.
Cattle weren't stirrin', fact they's
bunched against the cold.
The tack was hung near the
chuckwagon with care.
Why, we didn't know Santy was
close anywhere.
Cowboys on the ground were
wishin' for their beds
While nightmares of wild steers
ran through their heads.
'Tween now and the next gather,
we needed a nap.
Cookie had just finished, and
tied down the flap.
When out past the cavvy, there
rose such a fuss,
I sprang to my feet, leavin'
the bedroll a muss,
And grabbin' my shotgun and my
ragged ol' hat
I run t'ward the racket thinkin'
"…what'n thunder's that?"
When thoughts of amazement
through my head courses,
It was a buckboard teamed up
with draft horses,
A driver in red buckskins, so
spry and dainty,

I know'd in an instant, it
must be old Santy.
Quicker than jackrabbits, them
horses they came,
And, he's shoutin' commands to
each one by name...
"Get a step, Joe! One more, Prince!
On, Big Ed!
Pick it up, Sam! Tighten up, Lou!
On, Old Ned!
Don't spook the cavvy, back away
from them pens,
You're a pullin' this wagon like a
bunch of ol' hens!
Now, when I haul on these lines
I mean to stop.
Hold up in this cow-camp like a
ton of cow flop!"
They sat down in their riggin',
like I knew they would,
With a wagon of goodies...made
of leather and wood.

Then, in a twinklin' with no
further delay,
He said, "Back it up, boys, this
here ain't no sleigh."
I couldn't believe my ears,
and lookin' around,
Off that wagon ol' Santy came
with a bound.
He was short, and his chinks
reached near to his toes.
He was happy and fat, with
a little red nose.
There was a ton of packages
and some new tack,
And, ol' Santy was carryin' it
all on his back.
His eyes sort of bloodshot,
much like a cherry,
From 'rastlin' them horses
clean across the prairie.
His lips was plumb puckered,
his mouth drawn and droll.
(Mine got that way, the day I
swallowed my Skoal.)
He was holdin' a piggin' string
tight in his teeth,
Nor fer' tie down, but tyin'
'up' a fine wreath.
His head was too big and he
had a round belly,
No doubt derived from eatin'
Texas Chili.
He's chubby and plump all right,
I'd say quite jolly.
I laughed plumb out loud when
I seen him, by golly.
He winked his bloodshot eye,
and spat 'tween his lips,

And, it made me to know we
were all in the chips.
He weren't much for chatter,
just done what was due,
Givin' presents and goodies
to the whole durn crew.
Then, he stuck his finger in
his wee little ear,
Wallered it around and said,
"We're through bein' here."
He fled to the wagon, and his
team called 'em up,
"Come on you swaybacks...what's
the dad-burn holdup?
We won't be back till next year
'cause we're flat broke.
Merry Christmas, my eye,
I just busted a spoke!"

From
http://www.humorspace.com/humor/
holidays/ccowboy.htm
David Kelley calls this "My Cowboy's Night
Before Christmas" because, he says, just
about every cowboy poet he knows has a
version of this well-loved poem.

Dusty Dancing

by J. Evetts Haley
Tascosa, Texas, 1888

The weekly and then semi-weekly arrival of the mails, with the coming of mule and oxen trains, always caused a flutter among the Tascosans, but the session days of district court, July the Fourth, and Christmas always caused considerable stir.

All the cowboys came in at Christmas. The fiddler resined his bow and, with head thrown back and foot a-patting, played "Turkey in the Straw," "Arkansas Traveler," "Goodby, Old Paint," "Cotton-eyed Joe," and other such favorites. At frequent intermissions the dancers left the ballroom of the Russell Hotel while the dirt floors were sprinkled down and the fog of dust settled.

From *Old Tascosa:*
The XIT Ranch of Texas
The formation and expansion of the largest ranch in Texas, 3 million acres supporting longhorns and mustangs, influenced the course of Texas history. Sprawling acres once roamed by Indians, buffalo, and antelope became oil fields and prosperous farms.

Hoppy's Fried Chicken

This is a fine recipe that will be utterly ruined if you cook the chickens over too hot a flame.

2	young chickens, 1 1/4 pounds each
	salt and pepper
3 cups	flour
2	strips bacon
1 pound	butter
1 1/2	cups whole milk
	parsley

Cut up the chickens. Wash and drain, but do not wipe dry. Season with salt and pepper. Roll in flour. Fry out the bacon until there is deep fat in the pan. Add butter and chicken. Cook slowly in hot fat, turning frequently until chicken is well browned.

Remove chicken to a hot platter. Add bacon and milk to the cooking fat. Stir thoroughly. Let simmer for 15 minutes. Pour over chicken. Garnish with parsley.

From *Hoppy Talk: The Newsletter of the Official Hopalong Cassidy Fan Club*

As Hopalong Cassidy, actor William Boyd was beloved as one of the Silver Screen's and TV's greatest cowboy heroes of all time. He and his horse, Topper, made sixty-six Hoppy films before the popular television series (with a total of ninety-nine episodes) started in 1948.

Mrs. Trouble

by Mary Kidder Rak
Southern Arizona

During our very brief stay in town, I did all my Christmas shopping, which consisted wholly of tissue paper, seals, and string. This year I can see Christmas drawing nearer without a qualm. When I was last in California, Mildred taught me how to make hooked rugs and Theodore made a hook and gave it to me. To one as impecunious as I, it is delightful to be able to make Christmas presents by combining old barley sacks and worn-out silk stockings. I am becoming a nuisance to my friends by reason of letters importuning them to send me their cast-off hose. There is a fine graft to it which I am keeping dark. My town-dwelling friends discard their silken hosiery for just a trifling run or two. The cows do not notice such small defects and I amble around the corrals on silk-clad feet. I feel so much more at home in cotton ones with a patch on the heel that I am reminded of the story of one of our jovial neighbors. He once told us that as a boy he was so hardened to going barefooted that when he had his first pair of shoes he had to put some gravel into them before they felt comfortable.

In addition to the hooked rugs, made during evenings spent beside the blazing hearth-fire, I shall send away the Christmas gifts which I annually pluck from the trees. In the early part of December I begin prowling around in the forest, looking for the trees which promise the most beautiful clusters of mistletoe. Imitating its host, the parasitic plant bears a resemblance to the tree it grows upon. On the oak tree it offers a profusion of white, waxen berries and small, curled leaves. On the sycamore, the mistletoe clusters have loosely sprawling foliage and berries of a deep cream color; while the pink berries of the juniper mistletoe grow on tight clumps of green that resemble needles more than leaves.

Just before Christmas each year, I place my boxes in a row and line them with tissue paper. Then we go out into the woods to gather the mistletoe and the gray-green berries of the juniper as well. As the car bumps over its annual route up the pasture to a sheltered glade where the greens grow profusely, the eight-feet-long pruning-knife, which we call the "long-legged snicker," jounces on the fenders. When we reach up into a tree with it and nip off a high-growing mistletoe, "snick, snick!" the Christmas presents fall on the ground. It is like shaking a breadfruit tree.

In only one year we knew a scarcity of waxen berries, when the mistletoe suffered from unusually heavy autumnal frosts. Our touring car was out of commission for some reason; Charlie was away and I do not drive the truck. Taking the long-legged snicker on my shoulder, I trudged the length of the home pasture and up to the sunny hillside which offered the only mistletoe growing near-by that had escaped the frost. When I had cut cluster after cluster, I made them up into large bunches which I tied together with strong twine. These bunches I tied in pairs so that I might carry two at a time without losing any of my cargo; one pair at a time I carried down the hill toward home. When I grew so tired with the weight that I could carry it no farther, I deposited my green and waxen burden on the ground and went back for more, resting myself by relaying the heavy mistletoe. Very gratefully I picked up the last two bunches and walked down the rocky hill on my final trip. I still had to pick up the greens, which I had left in a pile about halfway home, but the walking would be smoother and easier.

As I approached the spot in the pasture where I had deposited my greens, I caught sight of a familiar bulky, black cow, all too near my pile of mistletoe. I ran. I shouted with all the breath I could spare—quite futilely.

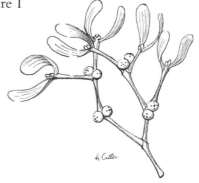

Mrs. Trouble, her big hoofs planted in the midst of broken greens and trampled berries, had eaten up the Christmas cheer.

From *A Cowman's Wife*
The adventures and misadventures of a young couple struggling to make a living from their cattle ranch in the shadow of the Chiricahuas Mountains of southern Arizona.

When Cowboys Were Boys

by Katie Kidwell

You know, I've got some real fine memories of Christmas. Now when Christmas comes, and I'm snowed up and alone in some line shack feeding cattle, I get those memories out and have myself a grand old time remembering.

Used to be when I was a boy we always had something happening and I remember one Christmas when the folks had to go into town to pick up some Aunt who'd just arrived from Boston. My sister was quite a rascal back then. Just as soon as they were gone we opened up both the front and back doors of the house and filled the floor between with a good layer of snow. Then we took our old sleigh up the hill which was right behind the back door and boy did we let her rip...right through the back door and out the front. Course we had to aim real careful or we hit the wall.

Sure was fun...of course we caught hell when the folks got back. I think my father got a kick out of it but he wasn't gonna let mother know. No, she wasn't all that fussy about the mess we made, that's for sure!

Yes sir, it sure is nice to remember Christmas when you're all alone somewhere listening to the wind howl. Kind of puts the sound of church bells and carols into your soul just thinking about it.

From *The Cowboy's Campfire in Cyber Space*
Katie Kidwell lives on a ranch in the Cariboo and has a fascinating Internet Web page about cowboys and ranching at http://www.cariboolinks.com/kidwell.

Gunman's Christmas

by Caddo Cameron
The Nations, Oklahoma

Meanwhile we're all busy as prairie dogs. I take the liver, heart, sweetbreads and a slice of tenderloin from the buck and make us a larrupin' son-of-a-gun stew for supper, and Arkansaw he fixes a dried peach cobbler that's big enough for two meals, and Kansas goes to a pool downriver that I tell him about and comes back with a dozen big catfish for breakfast Christmas mornin', and Choctaw sees a cottontail and right away decides he wants a rabbit stew for eatin' sometime today—he ain't particular when—so he takes the bow and arrows again, and comes back with six rabbits, and durned if I ain't makin' another stew before I know it. I reckon men on the dodge eat more than other men when they get a chance. With the law sniffin' and a-growlin' at your hocks, if you stop to eat you won't live to eat.

Watchin' me and Arkansaw a-mixin' this and that, Choctaw wants to know, "Where did you ever get all this fancy stuff away out here? White flour, long sweetening (sorghum), short sweetening (white sugar), canned milk, spices, onions, sweet potatoes, lard, and all kinds of dried fruit. Where did you ever get it?"

I look at him. "Personal question, Choctaw, and nobody but a durned fool ever answers a personal question."

Choctaw allows he's plumb sorry and Arkansaw says he'd ought to be, and then everybody laughs fit to kill, and I'm thinkin', company for Christmas ain't a bad idea.

The big event of the day, as a fella says, comes when I put the turkeys down to cook. It's full dark and everybody is there and I reckon nobody is thinkin' about gunfightin' and killin' and the law and hangin's and such, 'cause all we're talkin' about is this here turkey bake. We've got a big bed of redhot coals in the pit. I mix me a clay mortar and plaster the gobblers, feathers and all, about three inches thick with the sticky stuff and lay 'em down there on the coals, then we cover 'em with dirt and build a slow fire on top of 'em and we stretch buffalo robes around it and the green deer skin over it to hide the glow.

When we're finished, I tell the boys, "Them turks ought to be about right for eatin' by tomorrow and that's Christmas."

Kansas is a-starin' into the fire sorta dreamy-like, and he says, "A Christmas dinner with all the fixin's."

Regardless of the fact that we play four-handed Seven-Up until midnight and don't sleep much after that, this fool Kansas rousts us out when it's comin' day on Christmas mornin'. Ain't he got a brain in his head, that kid. He swears he heard Santa Claus on the roof last night and I tell him that all he heard was Old Henry Clay a-crunchin' a packrat's bones, and Choctaw declares I lit in the middle of the floor with a six-shooter when the first bone popped and I tell him he's a liar, but Arkansaw swears it's so and dad-blame me if they don't mighty nigh convince me that it *is*.

Then Choctaw says, "As I told you, I'll give you twenty dollars to show us that draw of yours."

I shake my head, pourin' him some coffee.

"I'll make it fifty, cash, if you'll do it slow."

"Go to hell," I tell Choctaw.

That old temptation must have been workin' on him in his sleep, and I'm thinkin', Christmas don't look none too promisin'.

But a wallopin' breakfast of corn pone and fried catfish topped off with a middlin' big helpin' of leftover rabbit stew sorta smothers the temptation and Choctaw behaves right human for a while. He pitches in and helps Arkansaw and Kansas fry a stack of venison steaks to be warmed up in their gravy and go with the turkey, and I say I'll mix a bakin' of cush to go with both of 'em.

"What's cush?" asks Kansas.

"Cush? Ain't you never heard of cush? It's outlaw cake and I was brung up on it."

So I take some stale wheat bread and crumble it and mix it with corn meal and soak 'em in hot water, then I put in hot fat— bear fat will do—and

Buckskins and
blankets

(NA695-30)

some raisins 'cause I got 'em, and salt and plenty pepper, and I cook my cush
in a skillet until it's nice and brown and fit to go with any fat gobbler.

Meanwhile the boys are so wrapped up in fixin' our Christmas dinner,
nobody ain't offered to stand guard on the bluff and I don't say anything
about it. Damned careless, I know. But, to tell the truth, I reckon all of us are
burnt out on eternally standin' guard, asleep and awake, and we're mighty glad
to sorta forget the law and The Hangin' Judge for one day at least. Now that I
think of it—one of the best night's sleep I ever got, I got in jail. Next day I
busted out and didn't get no sleep for a week.

It ain't noways time for dinner, but the boys keep a-wonderin' out loud
whether them turks ain't burnt to a crisp and such talk—I'll swear they're like
kids—until I can't put up with it no longer, so I tell Kansas and Choctaw to
go and dig them gobblers up. There ain't a sign of a leak in their clay shells,
which makes me right proud. When we crack 'em open feathers and skin
come away with the shell and there's our turk, plumb juicy like Nature made
him. Nothin' gets away, not even the gobble, and his meat is a-fallin' from his
bones. I might nigh have to hold the boys' off with a six-shooter.

We set the table inside right stylish and the boys' eyes pop out when I go to puttin' on a linen tablecloth and silver eatin' tools and English jams and jellies, but nobody asks me where I got the stuff.

Choctaw goes to his saddle-bags and finds two quarts of champagne. He gives 'em to me, sayin', "I've been saving these for Christmas. They've taken up room that I really needed for ammunition."

Arkansaw has been diggin' in his towsack morral. Up he comes with a pint of Old Crow, and hands it over. "'Tain't much, but it'll give us a taste of Christmas cheer."

Kansas fetches somethin' from his warbag. He looks sheepish and he talks thataway, too. "Here's a jar of wild plum jelly. A week or so back a squatter's old lady gave it to me for my Christmas dinner wherever I happened to be. Said she lost her own boy this time last year. Killed in a gunfight at Pond Creek."

Liquor and Old Temptation work in double harness and I'm afraid of what this team will do to Choctaw. I watch him close.

But he just sips a little champagne and stops at that and nobody else drinks much, which sets me thinkin' that if every man in this country was a gunsharp the anti-saloon preachers wouldn't have much to preach about. No gunfighter with a lick of sense will slow himself down by drinkin' when he's in fast company like this here Christmas gatherin' of mine.

I know we're a-celebratin' Christmas in a hole in the ground and the guns of the law may be linin' their sights on us for all we know, but we eat and talk and laugh and eat some more just like other folks do and I betcha we're havin' more fun than they do 'cause we ain't had a chance to celebrate thisaway since we were boys, maybe some of us never before. Kansas is havin' the time of his life. This sorrel-topped kid raises more Cain than any of us, and when it's gettin' dark and we build up a big fire in the chimney and shove the table out of the way and get our tobacco to goin' good, he starts to sing in that fine voice of his. Nobody talks then. Everybody listens—listens and thinks, I reckon.

Kansas sings about Christmas and happy folks who can show a light without fear of the law, and he sings of pretty things until my dingy old dugout commences to show spots of cheerful color, like bright curtains in place of a slab shutter on its window, and holly berries and mistletoe a-hangin' here and there, and a yellow tomcat a-sleepin' in front of the fire—his name was Slug—and over in the corner a little old cedar saplin' is all dressed up with red paper and cotton and red candles, and there's three pair of black stockin's a-hangin' on the tree, all of 'em darned a-plenty, and the longest stockin's are mine and—

Hell! I'm a-seein' things that I thought I'd done forgot. I go and pour me some coffee. Choctaw holds out his cup. He's got a faraway look in his eye. I wonder, maybe he's a-seein' things, too.

From *Gunman's Christmas*
In this poignant story by a prolific writer of Western short stories, four "anonymous gunmen," each with his own closely guarded secrets, come together to celebrate Christmas.

AC

Son-of-a-Gun Stew

1/4	of a fresh beef liver, cut in bite-sized pieces
1/2	of a fresh beef heart, cut in bite-sized pieces
	All the marrow gut, cut in bite-sized pieces
	All the sweetbread and brains, cut in bite-sized pieces
1 cup	chopped beef fat or paunch fat
1	large onion, chopped
1	small red pepper, chopped in small pieces
2	large carrots, chopped
2	sticks celery, chopped
3	cloves garlic (optional)
1 tablespoon	pepper
1 teaspoon	salt

Put all the ingredients except the brains in a large pot with 1 cup of water and bring to a boil. Skim off foam and continue cooking until all meat is tender, two to three hours. Add small amounts of water as necessary. Add the brains very slowly until the gravy is thick.

Stir often and cook as slowly as possible from the beginning.

This traditional cowboy dish is not for the faint of heart.

Boots and Canasta

In the 1951–52 Alden's Fall and Winter catalog, there is an ad for Hoppy boots at $8.95: "The official Hopalong Cassidy boot in softest black and white kid leather has fancy 2-gun stitching, bend-leather sole, sturdy, flexy Goodyear welt leather insole, pitched heel. Real cowpuncher style."[. . .]

Another catalog, the Sears 1950 Christmas Book, featured several Hoppy items, including a Hopalong Cassidy canasta set for $1.95. The description reads, "A thrilling new game for boys and girls. It's played just like adult Canasta, but the faces of the cards have 12 different colorful symbols of the West—picture of Hoppy and Topper on the back. Set includes 2 decks of cards, a score pad, rule book, and saddle-shaped revolving plastic tray. Postpaid. 1 lb. 8 oz. Or you could buy two decks of cards with instructions, no tray, for only $1.00 ppd."

From *Hoppy Talk: The Newsletter of the Official Hopalong Cassidy Fan Club*
Hopalong Cassidy, actor William Boyd, was one of Hollywood's best-loved cowboy heroes.

AC.

Line-Camp Christmas Letter

by S. Omar Barker

Inside an Old West line-camp, settin' on his lonely bed,
A cowboy wrote a letter home, and this is what it said:
"Dear Folks: It looks like Christmas time is comin' on again,
And I ain't wrote no letter since the devil don't know when.
So now I thought I'd drop a line just like I done last year,
To let you know I'm safe and well and full of Christmas cheer.
Seems like the news ain't much to tell. A blizzard blowin' now.
There'll be some cattle driftin'. Merry Christmas anyhow!
I've been out ridin' most all day. The horse I rode went lame.
The cattle sure are scattered. Merry Christmas just the same!
Last night my waterholes froze up. Snow sure is slow to thaw.
Some cattle lookin' porely. Merry Christmas, Pa and Ma!

Line-camp cabin in the Nicola Valley (Anne Tempelman-Kluit)

This line-camp shack has got some cracks that let the snow sift through.
Well, Merry Christmas to you, folks, and Happy New Year, too!
Excuse this crooked writin'. Got my hands frostbit, I guess.
The cattle sure are driftin'. Merry Christmas, Frank and Bess!
Ax handle busted. Woodpile low. Ain't got much fire tonight.
The drifts have knocked some line fence down. I trust you're all all right.
My pot of beans boiled dry and scorched while I was out today.
Them cows are driftin' awful. Merry Christmas anyway!
Well, folks, I've got to cut this short and mend my busted rope.
Just thought I'd drop a little line. You all keep well, I hope.
This cowboy life is wonderful. Sure glad I came out West.
Give my regards to Adelaide and Jack and all the rest.
I'm glad I ain't a cow tonight. Outside I hear 'em bawl.
Pore critters sure are driftin'. Merry Christmas to you all!"

From *Rawhide Rhymes*
Born in a log cabin at Beulah, New
Mexico, S. Omar Barker loved the area so
much that after his marriage in 1927, he
bought part of his father's homestead in
Sapello Canyon and had an adobe house
built in which he and his wife, Elsa, lived
for almost thirty years.

Baked Buffalo Calfs-Head

by Michael Steck

The Cook was also preparing one of their heads for our Breakfast. A Buffalo Calfs-head is considered a great luxury by the mountaineers. The following is the mode of cooking them. We dig a hole in the ground large enough to bury whatever is to be cooked, build our fire in and over it to heat the Ground & if the piece of meat is large such as turkey, Goose or Calfs-head we heat stones red hot and put them in the bottom, place the meat upon them and cover it over six inches deep with hot ashes then build the camp fire upon it and let it remain till morning when it will be finely cooked. Then with a stick you roll it out and remove the skin when it is ready to commence upon. I wish you could have been with us that morning, seated upon the ground around our Calfs-head. I know you would have been delighted with your breakfast and ready to join me in denouncing a roast, _____, a stew or fricassee so long as you could have a Calfs-head cooked as I have just described.

From "Trail Letter," *On the Sante Fe Trail*

Almost 1,000 miles long, the Sante Fe Trail stretched from Missouri to New Mexico, snaking across five states. Opened in the early 1820s as a trade route, the trail, a rough wagon road, traversed rivers, prairies, forests and deserts.

In winter, men and animals often died in the intense cold and snow storms, and travelers in the early years faced the ever present threat of attack by hostile natives. The arrival of the railroad in 1880 meant the end of the Trail.

Snowgirls

by Jack and Darlene Brown
Anahim Lake, B.C.

Even the children weren't immune from Pan's pranks. One year, Mary and Lisa Cassam rode over to the Home Ranch to spend Christmas with Diana, the girls all being near the same age. With not a lot to do in the snowed-in house, they began to badger Pan to take them for a sleigh ride. Came Christmas Eve and the weather warmed up a bit. Pan capitulated, but not wanting the bother to harness the team, he hitched up the hay sleigh to his tracked tractor, threw on some hay for the girls to set in, then picked up the squealing, giggling girls.

Pan put the tractor in gear and gave it gas. As they sped out into the meadow, he glanced back and saw the girls starting to hunker down in the hay. The tracks were picking up snow and throwing it back over the sleigh covering everything, including the girls in the sleigh bed. Pan "Hee hee"-ed and picked up speed. This threw the snow even harder and the girls began to yell for him to stop, but he pretended not to hear. The tractor, Pan, the sleigh with the screaming girls—all made a complete circle of the big meadow and then back into the yard.

When he stopped, three "snowgirls" rolled off the sleigh, completely covered with snow from head to toe. Pan thought it was hilarious, but the girls thought differently—on Christmas Eve the girls' sleigh ride had been a perfect setup for Pan.

From *The Legend of Pan Phillips*

By the time he was fourteen, Floyd Eugene Phillips had ridden almost everything on his father's Illinois farm, including the rams, and entertained his friends with "Wild West shows." Perpetually broke, he was given the nickname Panhandle because he was always bumming cigarettes. He left home to work on the wheat harvest in Kansas and cowboyed on various Wyoming ranches, always dreaming of owning a ranch.

Phillips decided that northern B.C. was a land of opportunity and when he met Richmond P. Hobson, Jr. in Wyoming, the two teamed up and headed north. Their story is told in Hobson Jr.'s book, *The Grass Beyond the Mountains*. Phillips, described as hawk-nosed, bowlegged and tough as rawhide, became a legendary cattleman in North America. Panhandle died in 1983.

The Bachelor's Turkey

by Susan Ames Vogelaar

Harold Butcher was a bachelor,
A proud and independent man.
No woman graced his kitchen,
Nor washed or wiped his pans.

He ran his cattle ranch alone
In the hills south of Pincher Creek.
He managed both ranch and home,
A woman companion he didn't seek.

Christmas season was coming
And his turkey was getting fat.
He planned a dinner for the single boys
He'd even put out the welcome mat.

When the fellows rode into the yard,
The turkey was almost done.
He made sure they were aware
He'd prepared it without anyone.

No woman's advice was needed
To cook up this magnificent feast.
He peeled and cooked the potatoes
And prepared all of the treats.

The turkey was golden and steaming.
The carving knife was sharpened with care.
Everyone gathered around
And pulled up their favorite chair.

Harold was about to prove
That women weren't needed here.
To those men waiting for dinner
That fact was certainly clear.

The first slice was juicy and tender
As it was laid upon the platter.
The second slice was placed on top,
But there was something the matter.

One of the boys saw something strange
Where the stuffing should be.
The entrails of the beast were revealed
For all of the guests to see.

There was no bread stuffing
With raisins and apples inside,
Just a bunch of intestines
With yesterday's dinner entwined.

The stench from those innards
Caused faces to turn a shade of green.
This was the strangest turkey dinner
That they had ever smelled or seen.

Harold had swore no woman was needed
To prepare and cook his meals,
But maybe he should have asked one
Cause those innards had no appeal.

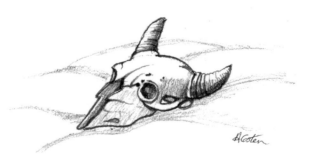

The feast had lost a bit of its flavor
But the guests were somewhat kind.
The ate up the potatoes and gravy
But that turkey was put aside.

The dogs were happy that Christmas,
They had an unexpected treat.
The bachelor's turkey was sumptuous
The entrails and the rest of the meat.

Now somehow this story was leaked
To the ladies who were not there.
Seventy years later, this story is still told
About the bachelor's Christmas fare.

From *Bards in the Saddle*
Inspired by the Cowboy Poetry gatherings
of the U.S., cowboy poets from Alberta
decided to form their own association in
1988. The association has flourished, and
this book includes poetry from Alberta,
Saskatchewan, British Columbia,
Yukon/Northwest Territories and
Montana.

A Country Dance

by Diana Palmer
Heffley Creek, B.C., 1920s

It was a perfect winter night. The air was clear and still, and a pale winter moon hung in the sky. We were off to the Christmas concert. The team was hitched to the big sleigh and we admired Dad sitting up in the driver's seat as he swung into the driveway. We waited at the kitchen door: our mother with Ross, now about two years old, in her arms, Martyn just home from boarding school for Christmas, and David and I, the *stars* of the evening. [. . .]

Off we started, with the jingle of sleigh bells, the squeaking of the runners on the packed snow and the howling of coyotes far off in the still night. It was 20 degrees below zero Fahrenheit, and we were bundled up in our warmest clothes. Dad had padded the sleigh box with sweet alfalfa hay, under which were heated stones—we four children sat here. Mother was up on the seat beside Dad, wearing her old fur coat and hat, with a wool blanket wrapped around her. She offered to hold Ross on her knee. But no way—he was having too much fun in the back.

We drove through the woods, under the snow-laden trees, and out on to the open range. The moon shone with the clarity of daylight. The team was hot. Steam rose from them and the whiskers around their mouths and nostrils were white with frost. The woolly scarves around our faces were also white with frost.

When we arrived at the school, Dad tied the team in a little stand of trees for shelter; other horses were tied nearby. We couldn't wait to show Martyn and our parents the glory that awaited within. We hurried into the school.

Under the guidance of Miss Bennett, our wonderful and resourceful teacher, we had been practicing for the concert for some weeks. Our post mistress, Kay Bedard, had been there often to play the piano while we practiced our carols. Local men came in each year to build a platform at the front of the school. The school enrollment, on an average, would be 10 to 12 pupils. Within the last day or two, we, the students had decorated the school and the Christmas tree.

As we walked into the school this night, to our eyes it was magnificent—

lights on, glistening decorations, and the sweet smell of pine and fir. Showing it to our parents filled us with great pride and joy. Looking at their faces, we hoped to see signs of utter disbelief at the beauty of it all. They complied, with their gasps of wonder that "it could be even better than last year!"

The evening was off to a good start; carols sung, recitations said, and some nifty play acting performed. We touched on Shakespeare, Robin Hood, and Sir Walter Scott's *Lochinvar*. From ranching country, we all liked the latter: "Young Lochinvar rode out of the west. On all the wide border, his steed was the best."[. . .]

Mike Spitco, a new boy in school, had, with his parents, recently immigrated from Poland. [. . .] His face was pleasant and tanned, his eyes blue, his teeth big and square. He spoke no English, but whistled loudly as he jauntily walked along.

Mike's happy whistle gave Miss Bennett an idea. She decided to have a *whistling trio* perform at our concert. [. . .] Although we got off to a good start things went awry part way through. Martyn, as ever a tease, was standing at the back of the room making faces at us. Halcyon and I were convulsed with giggles. Mike, with his head thrown back, strongly whistled on. He saved the day!

Polo Ponies

David   Diana

✿ A Merry Christmas and a Happy New Year ——

Santa appeared, ho-hoing his way through the crowded room, and gifts were handed out. There was a feeling of celebration. The concert had ended successfully with applause—certainly to us it was great and overwhelming applause.

Just as the concert was over we heard sounds of loud laughter and celebration, with many *yippees* and *yahoos* coming from the woods behind the school. The local boys had started to celebrate in anticipation of the dance that was to follow. In those early days they would have had a few crocks of boot-legged home-made wine stashed in their saddlebags. Among the drinkers there were three or four boys who had brought along musical instruments; usually a guitar, a banjo, a fiddle and an accordion. It wasn't unusual to see a young fellow riding through the night with a guitar or banjo tied to the back of his saddle. The *band* received no payment—not even a collection taken. The idea would have been an insult to these independent, carefree ranch boys.

In preparation for the dance, the school desks were pushed back against the walls—seat side out. Toddlers and babies were put to sleep on the desk tops, which were snug against the wall. Ross spurned this suggestion, he would much rather dance. Little kids did whirl around the floor amongst the adults, and really did enjoy the dance—especially unshy ones like Ross.

The fun of the dance was not always the reason for attendance. It was a time to visit and sometimes do business. Deals were frequently made within the walls of the little school house. David and I both remember a time when Dad bought 40 head of cattle for $8 each. The owner had come with the express purpose of selling this small mixed herd. Not wanting to pass up a good buy, Dad wished to pay him immediately. A check was not to be found. A page from a scribbler was. Dad wrote it up in the form of a check and signed his name. I remember, as part of the deal, the cattle were to be picked up by the buyer—no easy task. They were on a remote farm in a thickly wooded area, and headed up by a few old lead cows who did not wish to leave home country!

Well, back to the party! The women were preparing food in the school basement. Everyone had brought something special and shortly supper would be served.

The band especially enjoyed Christmas concerts because there was a platform on which to stand. Instruments were soon tuned up and the little school house was rocking! Fast dances, slow dances, square dances—there was always a good *caller*. The girls sat hopefully along the walls. The boys, standing in a group near the door, at the first beat of the music, stampeded over to ask for dances.

The band was in high spirits, often bursting into song, yodels or more *yippees* and *yahoos,* sweat was pouring down their faces. Beatles, eat your hearts out! A few short breaks were taken to breathe in the cold night air, and perhaps a quick trip to the saddlebag. I must explain here that none of these boys were serious drinkers. It would have been unheard of. Only a bit of light celebration for dances took place. No unions here—they played on to the wee small hours.

Long before this, however, parents were bundling up their children and herding them out to the sleighs. The sound of welcoming nickers could be heard from our patient team. All aboard and snuggled down in the hay, we were soon on the trail for home. Pulling away from the school, we heard the loud beat of the music accompanied by the even louder rhythmic thump, thump, of the dancers' feet. A country dance sound, long to be remembered with nostalgia.

From *A Ranching Family— Snapshots & Memories*
This book details the history of a large British family who first settled in Toronto, Ontario in 1836. Their daughter, who married and settled in Victoria, British Columbia, had eight children. One of them was the father of Diana Hett Palmer, who wrote this book about her family adventures ranching on Heffley Creek near Kamloops in the 1920s.

In 1857, 16-year-old Joseph Guichon left France to join his three brothers and prospect for gold in the Cariboo. The brothers soon became involved in other ventures. In 1882, Joseph settled at the mouth of the Nicola River and founded the Home Ranch.

By 1890, the Guichon Cattle Company was the largest operation around, with 2,000 head of cattle. Joseph died in 1921, but the property has remained in the family. Gerard Guichon now owns the northern properties, and Guy Rose owns the southern sections, including the Quilchena Hotel.

Brandy

by Bob Kinford

There are cow dogs and then there are COW DOGS and Brandy was one of the latter. She would work either end of a cow nipping the heels of a slow-moving steer or grabbing the ear of a wild runaway. She had helped me gather four hundred steers out of a five-section pasture in one day (we only missed one) and pen cattle into corrals with the only gates on the outside corners. If I needed to count cattle through a gate all I needed to do was start them through, then sit back and count, as she would push them through while I counted.

When I moved into town to train horses she would follow me everywhere I went. If I left in a friend's vehicle and left her home she would be waiting in the back of the truck when I returned. On the rare occasion I took my truck somewhere and left her home she would always be waiting for me faithfully at the door when I returned.

Then two days before Thanksgiving a couple of friends stopped by to take me out to dinner. During dinner a fierce wind came roaring in out of the north destroying anything which wasn't nailed down. When I returned home a small metal shed had been blown apart and pieces of the barn roof were gone, as was Brandy. The wind was blowing too hard to call her so I looked in the barn and around the farm but for the first time in the six years I had her she was gone.

For the next two weeks I searched daily. My dogs come to my whistle better than their name so I would take the colts I was riding and search along the river and down side roads I had never been on, whistling for her as I rode. Every time I saw a Blue Heeler from a distance I would have to get a closer look. After two weeks I had to concede that my faithful companion of the last six years was gone. What had happened I could only speculate upon.

The wind and blowing tin must have terrified her so badly that she ran away, but then what? I knew she had not been killed by a car because I would have found her body, unless she had managed to crawl into the brush to die. She had not been taken to any of the local veterinarians or to any animal shelters. I would never know the final resting place of my faithful companion.

The night before Christmas Eve I went to a party with my friend Rachel and when we returned there was a message on her answering machine for me. It was my landlady, who lived next door to me.

The message was, "Bob, there are a bunch of dogs on the porch and I think one of them is Brandy!"

I jumped in my truck and drove straight home and was greeted by none other than Brandy herself, squirming on her side, thumping her tail and literally grinning from ear to ear! It was as if the other dogs had brought her home for Christmas, for like Santa, they were nowhere around.

I wish dogs could talk so that she could have let me know what had happened to her. She couldn't use one back leg and was a virtual skeleton from having to fend for herself while being hurt.

The next day as I rode she was there in her usual place, sitting in the middle of the arena just watching me ride around. I guess miracles do happen around Christmas time, don't they?

From *Cowboy Romance:*
Of horse sweat and hornflies
Wry, dry and witty, Kinford's recent fictions are tongue-in-cheek cowboy adventures, both the "Hollywood" kind and the less romantic blood and sweat sort. For more see http://www.2lazy4u.com/cr.htm

E.P. Ranch Christmas Cake

by Chef Bob Bradley

1 cup	dates
1 cup	boiling water
1/4 cup	butter
1 cup	white sugar
1	egg
1 teaspoon	vanilla
1 1/2 cups	all-purpose flour
1 teaspoon	baking powder
pinch	salt
1 teaspoon	baking soda

In a saucepan combine dates and water. Simmer until dates are soft and have mixed with the water.

Cream the remaining ingredients, except baking soda, in a large mixing bowl.

When dry ingredients are ready, add baking soda to dates and water, keep on heat for about 10 seconds or until mixture becomes puffy. Combine the two mixtures, mix well and pour into a 9" square cake pan. Place in a 350°F oven for 30 minutes.

Note: Date mixture may be dry, just add a little more water if necessary.

E.P. Ranch Christmas Cake Icing

by Chef Bob Bradley

1/2 cup	brown sugar
5 tablespoons	butter
1/2 cup	coconut
3 tablespoons	cream
1/2 cup	chopped walnuts

In a small saucepan heat the sugar, butter, coconut and cream.
Once heated through, add the walnuts.

Remove from heat and spread evenly over the E.P. Ranch Christmas Cake.

Place under HOT broiler or salamander for about 45 seconds or until mixture starts to bubble.

Serve warm with strawberry preserves and whipped cream.

Note: Be careful not to burn icing when broiling.

 From *Buzzards Cowboy Cuisine, Calgary, Alberta* and *The Wild West Cookbook*
The EP Ranch, south of Calgary, certainly has one of the most colorful histories of the Alberta ranches. Started in 1884 on Pekisko Creek, the ranch caught the eye of Crown Prince Edward during a visit in 1919. The Prince of Wales purchased the 4,000-acre ranch and renamed it EP (for Edward Prince). He owned the EP for 43 years, visiting three times during the 1920s, sometimes traveling incognito as "Lord Renfrew."

Edward became king in 1936, but abdicated a year later to marry Wallace Simpson. While Edward loved cowboys and ranch life, the new Duchess of Windsor preferred a suite at Calgary's Palliser Hotel.

Solitary Drive

by Fred Nichol
Knutsford, B.C., circa 1915

Christmas was simple in those days, but I think everybody celebrated it by taking a rest, all but my dad—he'd hitch the team up and go driving Christmas Day, alone—he never took anyone else. He'd give the horses a big feed of oats first, for their Christmas dinner, then he'd go for a ride.

Everyone had a lot of unemployed roosters in the winter—that was the Christmas dinner. A couple of roasted roosters, a big plum pudding, and maybe a little drink of wine, and everybody enjoyed it. Not too many people dropped in or out, except for several bachelors who lived close. I don't remember how many Christmases little Evan Roberts was at our place for dinner—him and Davy Jones.

We had a tree, all home decorated—we made the decorations out of tinsel paper; no lights on it except a candle or two—you had to be careful with them. The tree went up the day before Christmas—the day after, it was taken out.

From *Bunch Grass to Barbed Wire*
Reflections and recollections of the
ranching families who settled around
Knutsford, the rolling hill country
between the Thompson and Nicola
valleys just south of Kamloops.

Christmas in the Rimrock

by David Lavender
Colorado, circa 1920

Scuds of snow swirled down now and then, but not until late December did it storm in earnest. Then on the morning before Christmas we woke to find a foot of fluffy white on the ground. We got busy. We were running short of hay and had to move the huskiest cows out of the feed lots onto the range as soon as we could.

At dawn we crossed the river on the bridge above the ranch and turned the herd up a crooked old mine trail. It was slow traveling, and the afternoon was running out when we let the cows go in Saucer Basin, a shallow declivity spiked with sandstone monoliths lying far above the junction of the rivers. We had to ride clear across the basin to the Dolores rim to shut the gate that blocked an exit on that side. We were cold and hungry. Snow slanted in long streaks on the wind, powdering the green-black cedars and giving a queer, ghostly look to the looming rocks. Half a mile away was shelter: an abandoned mine building crouched by the circular rim of orange-colored sandstone that lent aptness to the basin's name. We sometimes used the shack when working the mesa and had equipped it with bedding, a stove, and food.

But none of us suggested staying there. For now it was Christmas Eve.

Down in the rimrock there are, as far as cowboys are concerned, two unbreakable holidays each year, Christmas and the Fourth of July, with Election Day thrown in every other November for good measure. These festive dates you can celebrate as your mood dictates. Generally the program consists in doing nothing whatsoever. Until evening. Then the countryside bestirs. By automobile, wagon and horse the tide flows to the nearest town, where invariably a dance is scheduled.

Roy hauled out his dollar watch, shook it as always when he discovered it had again stopped running an hour after winding, and put it back in his pocket. We didn't need a watch, though. The sky showed plainly that we could not reach home if we rode back across the basin and followed the roundabout trail we had ascended.

Common sense pointed right to the shack. But if we slept there we would miss one of Christmas's most singular privileges. We would have to get up the next morning and ride home. We would not be able to yawn in the face of the alarm clock and then burrow back into our blankets with the luxurious knowledge that for once we did not have to rise in darkness and set the teakettle on the stove to thaw while we made ready for another day's work.

"I reckon it's got to be Shamrock," George said. The Shamrock trail (heaven knows why it was dignified by that sound Irish name) is a short cut which falls down the red wall of the mesa to the bench above the river junction. Traveling it is bad in summer; in winter, when snow and ice make footing slippery above the five-hundred-foot drops, it is plain folly.

But this was Christmas Eve, and that bench way down below opened the way home. Down Shamrock we went with just the tips of our boots in the stirrups, ready to leap clear if the horses fell. We were too scared to talk, too hurried to get off and walk. The only sound was the crunch of snow under the ponies' feet, the scrape of a piñon branch across our sheepskin coats.

And then we came to the ford over the river. When I saw the shape it was in I thought, "My God, if we had stayed in the Saucer we would at least be full of supper now."

Rolling ice stretched across the stream from bank to bank. It didn't look very solid. But it was too late now to follow the tumbled canyon to the bridge. Gingerly we urged the horses on the ice. Sure enough, it split open beneath us. Somehow the animals kept their feet as we dropped through into the belly-deep water. But now the ice which had been too weak to support

Inseparable twosome
(NA2476-2)

them proved too strong for the horses to push through with their chests. They had to rear on their hind legs and by striking and lunging with their front hoofs break out a channel. I don't know why they didn't upset with us. Christmas luck, I guess.

At the ranch we rubbed down our horses and grained them. I got an ax and called Martha. The sky had cleared a little, and the last glimmer of a lemon-yellow sunset lay on the cliffs. We climbed the rise back of the barn, hunting a Christmas tree for the baby. There were no spruce such as you buy in cities, but we found a fragrant piñon pine that was almost straight. While I cut it Martha broke off an armload of cedar boughs. Laden with blue-gray berries, they would make handsome garlands.

As soon as the baby was asleep we set up the tree in the living room of the cabin we occupied across the lane from the cowboys' bunkhouse. Then we brought out the ornaments we had made: shiny stars hacked from coffee can lids and black walnuts wrapped in lead foil we had been filching from the farmer's chewing tobacco since early fall. Extra foil we cut into "icicles." Colored yarn made festoons; snips of paper did for snow.

Hanging the decorations, we forgot that it was ten miles to the nearest neighbor's, twenty-two to the post office. And after we had gone to bed with our three cats curled up at our feet we lay awake for hours, whispering in the dark like a couple of kids who know that Santa Claus is on the way.[. . .]

We had our presents, a yearling baby and preparations for a fitting feast to keep us busy. The cowboys, however, were bored stiff with their long-anticipated leisure. They fired the bunkhouse stove to unbearable heat and stubbornly lolled around it, re-reading the month-old county paper, yawning, and paring their fingernails to the quick. They were waiting on their toes like sprinters when I rang the dinner gong.

We were just sitting down when a timid knock sounded on the door. I opened it to a furtive-eyed man, horribly hunchbacked. His odorous black hair fell in snarls below his shoulders. It was Ike (his last name we never knew), a hermit placer miner who had holed up for the winter in a cave down by the riverbank.

He said nothing, and for a moment I could not imagine why he was there. Generally Ike ran for cover when anyone approached him. Then I realized that even hermits can be lonely on Christmas. I invited him in. Martha brought out another plate, but we couldn't get him to sit down. He stood there in the center of the room, shuffling his feet and darting glances over his shoulder at the door, like a stray dog in an unfamiliar place. Finally Roy whispered, "Pay him no heed." We commenced eating as if he weren't around. Finding himself no longer the center of attention, Ike sidled by degrees into the vacant chair and with a grin of agonized embarrassment passed his plate.

After dinner—venison soup and roast turkey, mashed potatoes, squash, carrots, and stewed onions from the root cellar; golden sourdough rolls and strawberry jam; apple pie and ice cream frozen with ice chopped from the river—we pushed our old automobile out of its shed. But not even a radiator full of hot water was blandishment enough to soften the engine's stony heart. So we hitched a team of horses to the car. Up and down the lane we dragged it. At last the oil loosened a bit. The motor coughed, died. Up and down again. Another furious spin with the crank. This time success.

Ike slipped back through the leafless willows to his cave. The rest of us piled in the car and, passing the baby from lap to lap, slued and slithered up the snowy road.[. . .]

It was dark when we reached the settlement this Christmas Day. We went first to old Jeff Grable's to leave the baby. Three or four other cars were already there. Jeff never went to the dances, and it was his self-imposed duty to, as he said, "ride herd on the young 'uns while their folks kicked up their heels."

His bedroom was bedlam. Rolling delightedly about on his bowed legs was old Jeff. His fingers have been warped by frostbite, and his pointed white brows stick out like owls' tufts above his pale blue eyes. He shooed each mother out of the house as soon as her child was tucked into one of the impromptu beds. It was his claim that parents are a distraction and that he could quiet the children better without them. Apparently he was right. Within an hour the house was as still as a prairie dawn. Heaven knows how he managed.

Next we went to Rial Payne's general store. It was open—too much business in town for Rial to lock up, holiday or no. The women gathered around the dry-goods counter in front. The men drifted to the rear. There, throned on a barrel under the horse collars, Buck Murphy was holding court.

He was a huge man, Buck was, with great pouches under his eyes. He looked flabby, but in the hayfields or at the branding fire he could work any two men to exhaustion. The biggest cattle owner in the district, he directed the roundups when we all got together and gathered the animals that had strayed off their home ranges—it was all public-domain land, of course, but what with permits, custom, the lay of the terrain, and so on, each rancher had what he called "his" section. The winter ride always started the morning after Christmas, and we were seeking Buck out for instructions. In a voice astonishingly small for the amount of flesh behind it he told us where tomorrow's gather would be held on Tabeguache Mesa and the country each of us should cover.

At eight-thirty the dance got under way in the town hall. Despite the crowd that packed the raftered room, it smelled musty and unused. The huge round stove by the stage could not drive the chill from the corners. Nonetheless, most of the women were in flimsy gowns, selected from mail-order catalogs and almost as new as Fifth Avenue in style.

The men were less fashionable. Those who wore neckties were outnumbered by those who did not. There was a generous sprinkling of crinkly new overalls. "Dress-up pants" are expensive and the opportunities to wear them limited.

Benches line the wall. These are for the women. You don't waste time with your partner during intermissions. She selects a seat on one of the benches, to which she returns after each number. When a new piece starts there is a stampede for partners. The system has its advantages. You know where to find the girl with whom you want to dance. All you have to do is reach her first.

Not all the women dance. Those who can't just watch and gossip. "Puncture ladies," the cowboys call them, because their tongues are ever ready to prick some reputation.

Nor do all the men dance. Some group in the corners and talk crops and livestock. Others, the more tipsy, hang around outside the door. This is the place where all the fights start; where, if you are in the mood, you pick one of your own. Many riders are visiting town for the first time in months. A pint of whisky and a rousing battle are the best release for high spirits. After the necessary amount of wordage the opponents, followed by a gang of spectators, step around behind the building. It is all in fun. When the combatants see each other at the roundup tomorrow they will most likely be as friendly as ever. And a black eye or split lip is a mark of distinction.

Inside, the dance goes on unrestrained. Even Amy Luce is down from Lost Park. This is the first time in ten months that she has seen another woman. Mrs. Williams, who has twelve children, is outstepping everyone.

The orchestra is a four-piece affair—piano, fiddle, banjo, and saxophone. It is very bad. But it can keep time, and that is enough. There are fox trots and waltzes for the younger folk, but many of the pieces are quadrilles, square dances and Virginia reels. Pete Hubbard does the calling. He stands on a table, his shirt sleeves rolled to his elbows, the sweat pouring down his round, wrinkled face. By midnight his stentorian bellow has sunk to a croak.

About one o'clock the arrival of old Jeff Grable causes a flurry. One of his charges is howling and will not be comforted. Jeff can't tell whose baby it is. So the mothers all rush down to his house, which the single malefactor has by now roused to a nerve-shattering uproar. What goes on inside, no mere male will ever know. But soon all is well and the women come trooping back.

At one-thirty there is a pie-and-coffee supper, served by the ladies of the Farmer's Co-op. The orchestra had been hired to play only until the supper, but a hat is passed and the weary musicians agree to continue.

Enthusiasm is waning, however. Most of the people have a long way to go to reach home. By three o'clock the last automobile has pulled away from the hall, and the town is a patchwork of black shadows in the frosty moonlight.

When we reached the ranch clouds had obscured the sky. Snow swirled in the yellow beams of the headlights. We were groggy with weariness as we put the car in the shed, drained the radiator, and carried the sleeping baby into the house. And in another hour we would have to be moving again, getting ready for the bitter ride to Tabeguache, for the long, long wait until summer.

But somehow we forgot all that as I lighted the lamp and the lead-foil ornaments gave back the flickering light. We stood there a moment looking at it. Then Martha said, "Let's keep it a little longer."

So I built a fire and we sat there, watching the tin stars twinkle on the branches.

Then pretty soon Martha said, "You'd better put the teakettle on the stove."

And I said, "Yes, Christmas is over."

From *One Man's West*

Initially interested in mining, David Lavender quickly switched his attention to cowboying. Cattle, cowmen and vast ranches, the uranium boom, prospectors and miners all play their part in this absorbing story of the American West and how it began to change more than half a century ago.

A New Year's Christmas

by Hughie Call
Madison Valley, Montana, circa 1920

That first Montana Christmas was celebrated the day after New Year, because I had stupidly put off holiday shopping until the roads drifted in. Tom warned me—as much as he ever warned me. Early in November he suggested that it might be a good idea to go to Butte and do my shopping. I put him off because I was anxious to see a play which was advertised to appear in a Butte theater sometime in December. I thought I'd kill two birds with one stone, and I killed them, all right—in reverse—for I didn't see that play and I did no Christmas shopping.

Two days before we hoped to leave a blizzard swept the Valley. For three days it blew and when its force was spent, we were snowbound. I had no gifts for Tom, the cook or the ranch men. Our Christmas box from Texas was in the post office, fifteen miles away, and there it would stay until we could dig our way to it.

Tom didn't mind for himself; it wasn't the first Christmas he had missed, but he was sorry for me. Two weeks before I had bought some tree ornaments at the drugstore in our nearest town. Tom insisted that we at least set up and trim a tree. This was a mistake. Each time I looked at those gaudy tinseled branches, a lonely red-and-gold box reproached me. True to the custom of the country, Tom had done his shopping early. This experience taught me a lesson I never forgot....

From *Golden Fleece*

Hughie Call was unprepared for life as a new bride on her husband's Montana sheep ranch. She quickly learned that the care and feeding of 14,000 ewes came before all else. She coped with temperamental cooks, one with 12 canaries, and the occasional outlaw, bear and rustler.

Cariboo Christmas (song)

by Alan Moberg

Oh the cowboys have all stopped riding,
The lumberjacks and the mill workers all come home,
The truck driver put his big rig away,
And they've rolled up the streets and the stores.

Little children are all trying to sleep now
'Neath a blanket of a Cariboo sky.
Peace, everyone peace now,
Christmas in the Cariboo's night.

Chorus:
Merry Christmas to you from the Cariboo,
Good health and good life and good cheer.
Merry Christmas to you from the Cariboo,
To old and new friends far and near.
Merry Christmas to you and the best New Year too,
We wish from the Cariboo.

In the sky the stars twinkle brightly
And the highway is finally still —
What's that I hear in the distance,
Was it a choir or the ringing of a bell?

As the countryside seems to be waiting
And in a small church someone kneels to pray,
Filled with praise and thanksgiving
For the gift that was given this day.

Repeat Chorus

Alan Moberg has been a songwriter and
performer for more than 30 years. He
loves Western Canada and this affection
is reflected in his songs. He has
performed at the Williams Lake
Stampede, for which he wrote and
recorded a song by the same name.
Moberg has won three B.C. Country
Music Association Awards.

Holiday Messages

by H. "Dude" Lavington
Quesnel, B.C., 1957

In 1957 we got a new service that was a wonderful help to us ranchers and folks away back in the sticks. Denny Reid, John Boates, Bob Leckie and Jim Ritchie started a radio station in Quesnel, our faithful CKCQ.

There were many public service programs: Music from Other Lands, International Hour, Trading Post (where you could trade off most anything but your wife), hockey games (Foster Hewitt had nothing on Bob Leckie!), Community Club that gave us all the community doings for miles in every direction, and many more, as well as Quesnel advertising rather than Prince George ads. We got to know the owners and some operators quite a little and talked them into getting one of our favourite programs—"Music and the Spoken Word"—from Salt Lake City, with the Tabernacle Choir and organ.

There were church programs from all the churches. But most of all the regular message programs helped so much. These message services have been a great help to the folks out in the boondocks. Almost like the old party telephone that all the neighbours listened in on. That way you knew what everybody else was doing.[. . .] Thank you CKCQ, we all sure appreciated these public services.

Then there were two special programs—one of Christmas messages and more at New Year's. On one occasion we had a horrible Christmas Day. There was a storm Christmas Eve and the temperature dipped away down past the 50 below mark and was around 40 below all Christmas Day. A bunch of cattle I was feeding up at the meadow came down and, after doing all the other feeding and chores, I had to take them back up to feed. It was close to the Christmas message time around 12:30 noon when I was ready to go. I hated to miss all the Christmas messages so I took a radio and put it in a saddlebag on the saddle horn, turned it up as loud as it would go and went to cowboying. As the radio got colder it got fainter and towards the last I had to stop everything and listen with the radio right up to my ear. I got the last message and then hung the radio on a tree and went on with my cowboying.

From *Born To Be Hung*
Dude Lavington and his brother Art were born on an Alberta ranch but migrated to B.C. in 1930, armed with nothing but the determination to build their own ranch south of Quesnel. Using only an axe and a crosscut or swede saw, the brothers cleared land, built cabins, barns, even twenty-five miles of road and seventeen bridges, all in four months. Undaunted by their experiences with horses, cattle, wolves and floods, the brothers prospered.

Opposite (from *Winter Feeding* by Maxine Abraham): I have wonderful memories of my early years on the farm. I was too young to understand the hardships, but I remember vividly my "friends," which were all the animals—especially my horse.

How all the animals depended on us, particularly during the cold winter days. Every day Dad would have to load up the hay rack and work his way through the deep snow with the team to where the range cattle were kept. I would beg to go with him and he would give me the very important task of guiding the team while he unloaded the hay. I felt so important to be able to perform this task at such an early age. I would wonder how he managed to do this job without me when I was in school.

A Cowboy's Christmas Prayer

by S. Omar Barker

I ain't much good at prayin', and You may not know me, Lord —
I ain't much seen in churches where they preach Thy Holy Word,
But You may have observed me out here on the lonely plains,
A-lookin' after cattle, feelin' thankful when it rains,
Admirin' Thy great handiwork, the miracle of grass,
Aware of Thy kind Spirit in the way it comes to pass
That hired men on horseback and the livestock that we tend
Can look up at the stars at night and know we've got a Friend.

So here's ol' Christmas comin' on, remindin' us again
Of Him whose comin' brought goodwill into the hearts of men.
A cowboy ain't no preacher, Lord, but if You'll hear my prayer,
I'll ask as good as we have got for all men everywhere.
Don't let no hearts be bitter, Lord; don't let no child be cold.
Make easy beds for them that's sick, and them that's weak and old.
Let kindness bless the trail we ride, no matter what we're after,
And sorta keep us on Your side, in tears as well as laughter.

I've seen ol' cows a-starvin', and it ain't no pretty sight:
Please don't leave no one hungry, Lord, On Thy good Christmas night—
No man, no child, no woman, and no critter on four feet—
I'll aim to do my best to help You find 'em chuck to eat.

I'm just a sinful cowpoke, Lord—ain't got no business prayin'—
But still I hope You'll ketch a word or two of what I'm sayin':
We speak of Merry Christmas, Lord—I reckon You'll agree
There ain't no Merry Christmas for nobody that ain't free.
So one thing more I'll ask You, Lord: just help us what You can
To save some seeds of freedom for the future sons of man!

From *Rawhide Rhymes*
Growing up in New Mexico's Sangre de
Cristo Mountains, S. Omar Barker knew
firsthand about horses and cattle. His
poetry and books won him two coveted
Spur Awards from the Western Writers of
America, as well as several other awards.
"A Cowboy's Christmas Prayer" is
probably his most memorable poem, and
has been a Christmas classic for decades.
Barker died in 1985.

Permissions

Every effort has been taken to trace the ownership of copyright material used in the text. The editor and the publisher welcome any information enabling them to rectify any reference or credit in subsequent editions.

"Shepherds of the Range," reprinted courtesy of Mrs. Robert E. (Jodie) Phillips.

"The Winter Camp," reprinted courtesy of the Will James Art Company, Billings, Montana.

"Stubby Pringle's Christmas," © 1964 by Jack Schaefer, © renewed 1992. Permission to reprint granted by Harold Matson Co., New York, NY.

"The Bull Named Jimmy Hoffa," reprinted courtesy of the publisher from *Chilcotin Holiday* by Paul St. Pierre, Douglas and McIntyre, © 1984.

"Standing Alone in the Darkness," reprinted courtesy of Arthur Winfield Knight.

"Wagon Boss Chili," reprinted courtesy of Cinda Chavich.

"The Matador Dance," reprinted courtesy of Indiana University Press, Bloomington, Indiana.

"Drylander's Christmas," reprinted courtesy of Mrs. Robert E. (Jodie) Phillips.

"Snowberries," reprinted by permission of the publisher from *A Pioneer Gentlewoman in British Columbia: The Recollections of Susan Allison,* edited by Margaret A. Ormsby, (Vancouver: The University of British Columbia Press, 1976).

"Cowboy's Christmas," reprinted courtesy of Hugh Dempsey from *Christmas in the West,* © 1982.

"Blackwater Drive," *Nothing Too Good for a Cowboy* by Richmond P. Hobson, Jr., © 1955. Used by permission of McClelland & Stewart, Inc. The Canadian Publishers.

"A Fiery Celebration," reprinted by permission of the publisher from *A Tenderfoot in Colorado* by R.B. Townshend, University of Oklahoma Press, Norman, Oklahoma, © 1968.

"Son-of-a-Bitch Stew," reprinted courtesy of Cinda Chavich.

"Bear Sign," reprinted courtesy of the publisher from *The Log of a Cowboy* by Andy Adams, Corner House Historical Publishers, Gansevoort, NY, © 1975.

"Christmas Greeting," reprinted courtesy of The Tom Mix Museum, Dewey, Oklahoma.

"Harking Back," reprinted courtesy of the University of Nebraska Press, Lincoln, Nebraska.

"Three Wise Men," reprinted courtesy of Mrs. Robert E. (Jodie) Phillips.

"Boots," reprinted courtesy of the Will James Art Company, Billings, Montana.

"Braised Wild Boar with Roasted Pepper Honey Whiskey Sauce" reprinted courtesy of Chef Goettler at Normand's Restaurant, Edmonton, Alberta and Hog Wild Specialties, Mayerthorpe, Alberta.

"Wind and Weasels," *The Canadian Cowboy: Stories of Cows, Cowboys and Cayuses* by Andy Russell, © 1993. Used by permission, McClelland & Stewart, Inc. The Canadian Publishers.

"All Kinds of Bad Weather," reprinted courtesy of the publisher from *Lucky 7: A Cowman's Autobiography* by Will Tom Carpenter, University of Texas Press, © 1957.

"Prairie Oysters," reprinted courtesy of Cinda Chavich.

"Cattle Christmas," reprinted courtesy of Veera Bonner.

"Stage Fright," reprinted by permission of Pocket Books, a Division of Simon & Schuster, from *Happy Trails: Our Life Story* by Roy Rogers and Dale Evans with Jane and Michael Stern, © 1994 by Roy Rogers, Dale Evans, Jane Stern and Michael Stern.

"Christmas Horses," reprinted courtesy of Theytus Books and Shirley Lewis.

"My Cowboy's Night Before Christmas," reprinted courtesy of David Kelley.

"Dusty Dancing," reprinted courtesy of the publishers from *The XIT Ranch of Texas* by J. Evetts Haley, University of Oklahoma Press, © 1953.

"Hoppy's Fried Chicken," reprinted courtesy of the Hopalong Cassidy Fan Club.

"When Cowboys Were Boys," reprinted courtesy of Katie Kidwell.

"Boots and Canasta," reprinted courtesy of the Hopalong Cassidy Fan Club.

"Line-Camp Christmas Letter," reprinted courtesy of Mrs. Robert E. (Jodie) Phillips.

"Baked Buffalo Calfs-Head," reprinted courtesy of the University Press of Kansas.

"The Bachelor's Turkey," reprinted courtesy of the publisher from *Bards in the Saddle,* edited by Susan Ames Vogelaar, Hancock House Publishers, © 1997.

"A Country Dance," reprinted courtesy of the publisher from *A Ranching Family—Snapshots & Memories* by Diana Palmer, M. Hepburn & Associates, © 1994.

"Brandy," reprinted courtesy of Bob Kinford, © 1999.

"E.P. Ranch Christmas Cake and Icing," reprinted courtesy of Buzzards Cowboy Cuisine, Calgary, Alberta.

Text Sources

Adams, Andy. *The Log of a Cowboy.* Gansevoort, New York: Corner House Publishers, 1903. pp. 280–85.

Allison, Susan. *A Pioneer Gentlewoman in British Columbia: The Recollections of Susan Allison.* Vancouver, B.C.: University of British Columbia Press, 1976. pp. 24–25.

Atherton, Lewis. *The Cattle Kings.* Bloomington, Indiana: Indiana University Press, 1961. pp. 196–98.

Barker, S. Omar. *Rawhide Rhymes.* New York: Doubleday, 1968. pp. 3, 12, 95, 122.

Bonner, Veera. "Cattle Christmas," *Chilcotin: Preserving Pioneer Memories.* Surrey, B.C.: Heritage House Publishers, 1995. pp. 366–67.

Brown, Jack and Darlene. *The Legend of Pan Phillips.* Morton, Washington: The Times Journal Publishing Company, 1986. p. 109.

Call, Hughie. *Golden Fleece.* Boston: Houghton Mifflin, 1942. pp. 151–52.

Cameron, Caddo. "Gunman's Christmas," *Christmas Out West.* New York: Bantam Western, 1990. pp. 197–99.

Carpenter, Will Tom. *Lucky 7: A Cowman's Autobiography.* Austin, Texas: University of Texas Press, 1957. pp. 112–13.

Chavich, Cinda. *The Wild West Cookbook.* Toronto: Robert Rose, 1998. pp. 22, 84, 118.

Chittenden, Larry. *Songs of the Cowboys.* Compiled by N. Howard Thorp. 1908. p. 35.

Dempsey, Hugh A., ed. *Christmas in the West.* 1892.

Haley, J. Evetts. *The XIT Ranch of Texas, and the Early Days of the Llano Estacado.* Norman, Oklahoma: University of Oklahoma Press, 1953. pp. 197–98.

Hislop, Herbert R. *An Englishman's Arizona: The Ranching Letters of Herbert H. Hislop 1876–1878.* Tucson, Arizona: The Overland Press, 1965. pp. 150–52.

Hobson, Richmond P. Jr. *Nothing Too Good for a Cowboy.* Toronto: McClelland and Stewart, 1955. pp. 78–86.

Hoppy Talk. Hopalong Cassidy Fan Club. Winter 1994.

James, Will. "The Winter Camp," *All In the Day's Riding.* New York: The World Publishing Company, 1927. p. 159.

James, Will. *Lone Cowboy.* New York: Charles Scribner's Sons, 1932. pp. 44–45.

Kidwell, Katie. *Memories of Christmas.* 100 Mile House, B.C.: The Cowboys Campfire in Cyber Space, 1999.

Kinford, Bob. "Brandy the Christmas Dog," *Cowboy Romances: Of Horses and Hornflies.* Lakeside, Oregon: Too Lazy For You Livestock & Literary Company, 1998.

Knight, Arthur Winfield. "Standing Alone in the Darkness," *Christmas Out West.* New York: Bantam Western Books, 1990. pp. 97–100.

Lavender, David. "Christmas in the Rimrock," *One Man's West.* New York: Doubleday, 1943. pp. 291–98.

Lavington, H. "Dude". *Born To Be Hung.* Victoria, B.C.: Sono Nis Press, 1983. pp. 161–62.

Lewis, Shirley. *Stories and images about what the horse has done for us.* Penticton, B.C.: Theytus Books, 1998. p. 55.

MacConnell, Charles E. *XIT Buck.* Tucson, Arizona: University of Arizona Press, 1968. pp. 254–55.

Mix, Tom. Christmas Card, 1926. Dewey, Oklahoma. Tom Mix Museum.

Palmer, Diana Hett. "Christmas Concert," *A Ranching Family—Snapshots & Memories.* Saltspring Island, B.C.: M. Hepburn & Associates, 1994. pp. 122–28.

Rak, Mary Kidder. *The Cowman's Wife.* Boston: Houghton Mifflin, 1934. pp. 215–17.

Rogers, Roy and Dale Evans (also Stern, Jane and Stern, Michael). *Happy Trails: Our Life Story.* New York: Simon and Schuster, 1994. pp. 26–27.

Rosehill Farmers Institute. *Bunch Grass to Barbed Wire.* Knutsford, B.C., 1986. p. 195.

Russell, Andy. *The Canadian Cowboy: Stories of Cows, Cowboys and Cayuses.* Toronto: McClelland and Stewart, 1993. pp. 207–9.

Schaefer, Jack. "Stubby Pringle's Christmas," *Christmas Out West.* New York: Bantam Western, 1991. pp. 223-34.

Simmons, Marc. "Trail Letter," *On the Santa Fe Trail.* Lawrence, Kansas: University Press of Kansas, 1986. p. 29.

Siringo, Charles A. *A Cowboy Detective.* Lincoln, Nebraska: University of Nebraska Press, 1988. pp. 248–52.

St. Pierre, Paul. "The Bull Named Jimmy Hoffa," *Chilcotin Holiday.* Vancouver, B.C.: Douglas and McIntyre, 1984. pp. 94–95.

Townshend, R.B. *A Tenderfoot in Colorado.* Norman, Oklahoma: University of Oklahoma Press, 1968. pp. 135–36.

Usted, Iyam B. *Stock Growers Journal.* Miles City, Montana, 1893.

Vogelaar, Susan Ames. *Bards in the Saddle.* Surrey, B.C.: Hancock House Publishers, 1997. pp. 19–20.

Photo and Illustration Credits

Photos on pages 9, 30, 43, 71, 93, 116 appear with permission from the
  Glenbow Archives, Calgary, Alberta

Pony Express Card, courtesy of Harry Rogers, Chillicothe, Missouri.

Cowboy's Christmas Star, courtesy of Tom Hunter, Langley, B.C.

Boots, courtesy of the Will James Art Company, Billings, Montana.

Cows on the Trail, courtesy of Veera Bonner, Big Creek, B.C.

Bronco Rider and Hotel Christmas Card, courtesy of Guy Rose,
  Quilchena Ranch, Quilchena, B.C.

Cabin and trees in snow, photo by Anne Tempelman-Kluit.

Two riders on horseback in snow, courtesy of Diana Palmer.

Santas Riding Broncos Christmas Card, courtesy of Guy Rose,
  Quilchena Ranch, Quilchena, B.C.

Winter Feeding painting, courtesy of Maxine Abrahams, Calgary, Alberta.